Elizabeth Williams Champney

Three Vassar Girls in South America

A holiday trip of three college girls through the southern continent, up the Amazon,

down the Madeira, across the Andes, and up the Pacific coast to Panama

Elizabeth Williams Champney

Three Vassar Girls in South America
A holiday trip of three college girls through the southern continent, up the Amazon, down the Madeira, across the Andes, and up the Pacific coast to Panama

ISBN/EAN: 9783337197308

Printed in Europe, USA, Canada, Australia, Japan

Cover: Foto ©Andreas Hilbeck / pixelio.de

More available books at **www.hansebooks.com**

ON THE AMAZON.

IN SOUTH AMERICA.

A HOLIDAY TRIP OF THREE COLLEGE GIRLS

THROUGH THE SOUTHERN CONTINENT, UP THE AMAZON, DOWN THE MADEIRA, ACROSS THE ANDES, AND UP THE PACIFIC COAST TO PANAMA.

BY

LIZZIE W. CHAMPNEY.

ILLUSTRATED BY "CHAMP" AND OTHERS.

BOSTON:
ESTES AND LAURIAT, PUBLISHERS,
301-305 WASHINGTON STREET.
1885.

PREFACE.

The author would acknowledge her obligation for much of the data used as background to this story to Mr. Herbert Smith, author of "Brazil, the Amazons, and the Coast," and to the letters and lecture of her husband, as well as to the published books of Professors Orton, and Hartt, and Mrs. Agassiz, to the reports of Lieutenants Herndon and Gibbon, and to other standard works. The admirable illustrations, by Mr. Franz Keller, which form a prominent feature of the book, are reproduced from his excellent work, "The Amazon and Madeira Rivers."

L. W. C.

SAUDADE DE PALMEIRAS.

Aqui, sentada na musgosa pedra,
onde aurea parasita cresce e medra,
 es queço-me a scismar,
e contemplo em silencio os altos montes
que se estendem sem fim nos horizontes:
 vagas d'un grande mar.

Quem podéra isolar-se no teu seio
ó doce solidao, trazendo cheio
 de amor o coração.
e meditando á sombra das palmeiras
escutar o bramir das cachoeiras
 perder-se na amplidão.

Brazil.   Adelina Amelia Lopes Vieira.

CONTENTS.

I. THE START
II. THE VOYAGE
III. PARA
IV. A PALMER'S PILGRIMAGE
V. NEAR TO NATURE'S HEART
VI. THE FAZENDA DA SILVA
VII. QUEER FISH
VIII. ON THE TRAIL
IX. A JAGUAR HUNT
X. VICTORIA REGIA
XI. THE MADEIRA TROUBLE
XII. HELP
XIII. THE DELECTABLE MOUNTAINS.—CUZCO
XIV. IN THE HEART OF A VOLCANO

ILLUSTRATIONS.

	PAGE
Maud in her Studio	11
Delight Holmes	13
Maud buying the Sketch-Box	15
Professor Holmes	16
Victoria	17
Good-By	18
Five Thousand Dollars Reward	19
Brazilian Flag	20
Adieu	21
Heaving the Log	23
Maud and the Doctor	24
Senhor Silva	25
A Leaf from Maud's Sketch-Book	27
The Photographer, Mr. Jenkins	29
Diving for Coins	31
Birthplace of Josephine	32
The Professor fishing for Sea-Weed	33
Maud and Senhor Silva passing the Light-Ship	35
Ascending the Para River	38
The Assai Stand	40
Tropical Plants	41
Indian Girl	42
Carrying the Sick Child	43
Rocket Prayers	47
The Temple of Isis	53
Siphonia Elastica	57
A Rubber Settlement	59
After a Lizard	62
Manufacture of Rubber	63
Maud's Sketch in the Rubber Swamp	65
Mr. Jenkins takes the Girls into Confidence	66
In Confidence	71
Mr. Jenkins's Opponent at Cards	75
Old Crone spinning	77
Indian Idea of an Eclipse	80
Indians singing Mass	85
Child asleep in the Shadow of the Cross	91
Senhor Palacios' Valet	92
Javary Palms	93
Orchids	97
Head of Swimming Tapir	99
The Cottage at the Fazenda	101
Graciliano spearing Fish	107
The Pirarucu	108
Pedro returning from Fishing	111
Indian Child's Hobby-Horse	113
The False Priest	117
Canoeing in a Submerged Forest	120
Seeing them off	123
Pedro	124
The Professor at Work	124
A Giant of the Forest	125
Jaguar fishing	129
The Dried Leaves Animal	132
A Halt in the Forest	135
"A Ringing Shot pealed through the Air"	138
The Senhor reads and disapproves	143
The Professor botanizing	146
Tropical Foliage	147
Macaws	148
"I have had quite enough of that man"	150
Victoria Regia	151
Maud has a Suspicion	157

	PAGE
Theotino Cataract	161
Caldeirao do Inferno	165
Mouth of Latreal River, Madeira	167
Caripuna Indian hunting	168
Bark Canoe of Caripuna Indians	169
Indian Dogs	171
Mr. Jenkins reveals himself	175
Tapuyo Indian River Craft	177
Bolivian Merchant	179
Exaltacion	181
Sword-Dance	185
"Go!" Victoria exclaimed	186
Peru	191
Gates hewn in the Rock	197
Peak after Peak	199

	PAGE
Inca Huayna Ccapac	202
Inca Tupac Yupanqui	203
Inca Yupanqui	203
Spanish Monastery	205
Effigies	204, 207, 208
The Farewell Tree	209
The Apurimac	217
Andean Peaks	219
Pizarro on the Road to Cuzco	221
Chimborazo	224
Cotopaxi	225
Spanish America	227
The Hacienda Mirandella	231
Graciliano and the Letter	235

THREE VASSAR GIRLS
IN SOUTH AMERICA.

CHAPTER I.

THE START.

MAUD stood in her tiny studio, high up under the chimes of Grace Church, while below her Broadway surged like a turbid, restless river.

Maud had worked here unremittingly all winter, but now her Easter orders were filled, and the last lily-decorated banner had left her work-table. There were signs of spring in the parks, where the sod was green and the trees a blur with bursting leaf-buds; there were signs of spring, too, in the shop windows, furs having been packed away in camphor-gum, and suffocating feather trimmings replaced by crisp French flowers, and airy lawns and laces. The south wind blew softly,

"Then longen folk to gon on pilgrimages."

A great restlessness possessed Maud; her studio walls seemed to be closing in around her, and the migratory feeling which beats in the breast of the swallow woke in her heart, — she must *go* somewhere. Her life had grown monotonous and narrow; she was hungry for a glimpse of broader horizons. There was a modest little store before whose windows she always paused on her goings up and down Broadway, a trunk store, with a tempting array of steamer-chairs, sole-leather and canvas-covered packing-cases displayed upon the sidewalk, and tantalizingly suggestive bags and reticules, lunch-baskets and toilet-cases, wicker-covered flasks, Russia-leather hand-bags, and other oil-skin or rubber-cased paraphernalia of a strictly businesslike aspect, or dainty, satin-lined luxuries, reminding one how easy the march of civilization had rendered journeys which were once full of hardship and privation. On this particular morning, Maud had even entered the store, and had inquired the price of a particularly neat sketch-box. Her fingers lingered enviously over the useful and ingenious space-saving appliances, and she put it from her with a regretful sigh. Nearer home she had caught a glimpse, through a conservatory door, of rich tropical foliage, palms, tree-fans, and orange-trees, and memories of where she had last seen them in wild luxuriance came drifting thick upon her. Maud was lonely, too; her mother had taken her invalid husband abroad, and Maud had remained bravely at her post of duty, sending regularly the little drafts which purchased the rest needful to restore her father to vigor. Maud could not afford to take a vacation. If only some opportunity would present itself of combining travel and money-making! but nothing seemed at present more unlikely. She was not just the person for a companion to an invalid, or governess for unruly children. She thought of her two firm friends, Cecilia, studying music in Germany, and Barbara, happily married in England, and she was not greatly to blame if a little feeling of envy crossed her usually contented and self-reliant spirit. She looked out of her studio window straight up toward the sky, and she could see, far above the spire of Grace Church, a straggling flock of wild geese flying north. The long V line was broken, for they had come far and were weary of wing, and latterly their ranks had been thinned by the sportsman's gun; but the leader kept bravely on, with his beak pointed due north, as though he carried a loadstone in his breast instead of a heart. Maud stretched her arms as though they were wings, — had she stood on the parapet just outside the window she might have leaped off, the feeling that she, too, must fly, was so strong within her.

Just then a letter was slipped beneath her door. She looked at it for a moment without opening it. "If this letter contains any possible suggestion in the way of travel," she said, "I will accept it." Oddly enough this was just what the letter brought. It was from a Vassar friend, Delight Holmes, the daughter of a western professor. Maud remembered her as a shrinking little freshman, with light, fluffy hair, and beseeching eyes, whom she had helped and befriended in her own senior year at college. However, that was two years ago, and there had been time for Delight to blossom into more of self-reliance, and Maud opened her letter with a warm feeling of interest. It read as follows:

DELIGHT HOLMES.

"FOSSIL-LEAVES ON THE PARADISE, KANSAS.

"DEAREST MAUD, — There is really not much use in my writing, for we shall soon be in New York, but I have a proposal to make, and I want you to be thinking it over.

"Father has at last received the commission which he has so long desired, to make an expedition to the Amazon, and mother and I will accompany him to

South America. It will be the crowning work of father's life. His theories are already developed and his book half written; he only needs personal observation to correct mistakes and to add proof. It is very necessary that the book should be illustrated, and means have been provided for an artist to accompany the party. The compensation which father can offer, beyond travelling expenses, will only be five hundred dollars, and we shall be gone at least five months. I am ashamed to offer you so paltry a sum, but we know of no one else to ask. Will you come with us for the sake of friendship and the good time we will surely have together? We will sail from New York on Wednesday, the 15th.

"I must not neglect to say that the friend who has made this possible is Mr. Delavan, the father of my Vassar chum, Victoria Delavan. He is a very wealthy man, and has become interested in father through our friendship. Last week he sent us five round-trip tickets, supplemented by a generous check. Victoria's mother died last winter; she has been with us ever since, and is going out with us. Indeed, it is she who has engineered the trip. She is a magnificent girl, and I want you to know her better. I think you were scarcely acquaintances in the old Vassar days. Father is rather lame in Portuguese, and when I told him that you had been to Portugal, and understood the language, he declared that this was an additional reason why you must go with us.

"I am sure you have not the heart to disappoint

"Your friend, DELIGHT HOLMES."

Maud clapped her hands in her joy; a door of escape had been opened to her, and the very opportunity for which she had so longed, to visit new lands, presented at the same time. Her father and mother were visiting her sister Lily now. Lily was the wife of a naval officer, settled for a few years in a charming villa at Nice, the five hundred would be more than they would need for the coming season, and with her own expenses paid, what more could she desire? She hurriedly wrote to her parents, detailing the scheme, and quite sure in advance of the reply, stopped that afternoon at the trunk store, and secured the travelling sketch-box which she had so much admired.

Maud was right in expecting her parents' approval, for a cablegram was soon received announcing their consent. Professor Holmes was known to them personally as a man of the strictest integrity, and of

MAUD BUYING THE SKETCH-BOX.

cool-headed caution, and in Maud, herself, her parents had unlimited confidence. She was twenty, had twice travelled in Europe, was self-reliant and equal to any ordinary emergency.

Mrs. Holmes was a gentle, motherly woman, lady-like and refined, intelligent and self-sacrificing. It seemed to Maud, at first, that she was simply Delight grown older, with a square of black lace on the same light mass of curls; but as she came to study her friend, she realized that there was more to Delight than she had at first fancied. She possessed the good qualities of both her father and mother; with the sweet lovableness there was combined an eager, devouring love of study, which had swept the college curriculum, so far, as a river inundates the lowlands, but was destined to settle back into her own proper channel of botany. Already, Delight Holmes knew more about ferns than any other girl in America. She had a noble collection packed away in herbarii, in her father's study, and a number of the Vassar girls who had travelled had sent her specimens from foreign lands. This journey was, consequently, a grand opportunity for her as well as for the Professor, who was concerned principally in fossils and in the glacial period. Delight had also a third nature, peculiarly her own, marked by a sweet cheerfulness which the

PROFESSOR HOLMES.

most adverse circumstances could not dampen. There were dark days in store for them all, but through the gloomiest she shone like a " candle on a candlestick, giving light unto all that were in the house."

Professor Holmes was, of course, the centre and heart of the expedition. He had worked for it many years, and his face was aglow with the joy of a man who is about to grasp the prize of his life. Maud trembled when she saw how very frail he was; but he was full of energy and enthusiasm, his clear, gray eye shone with cheerful hope, and his voice had an exultant ring. He was eager to be off, and when the steamer really did sail, Delight said that her father would have leaned against the mainmast all the way if by pushing he could have helped it one inch upon its course.

Victoria Delavan was as yet an unknown quantity, and Maud eyed her curiously, not at all certain whether she would like or dislike. So far she had only shown herself a tall, languid girl, with beautiful eyes and an aristocratic nose; solitaires glittered in her ears, and she was expensively dressed in the latest Parisian styles.

Maud wondered whether a separate boat would be chartered to convey her wardrobe up the Amazons. In arranging her own wardrobe, Maud had acted on the principles governing a soldier preparing for a long march. So rigid had been her retrenchment that she had even had her hair closely cut, imparting a still more boyish cast to her frank face.

VICTORIA.

"No telling," she had explained, "but we may reach lands where hair-pins are not indigenous; and we may not be fortunate enough to encounter Fragoso, Jules Verne's wandering barber of the Amazons."

The appointed morning dawned brightly, and the party, escorted by a retinue of friends, found themselves on board the steamship "Advance," of the United States and Brazil mail line.

Those of Maud's acquaintances who were not on the wharf in Brooklyn had sent good-by gifts, and she had never realized her popularity so much before. Lotta Fanning sent a basket of pineapples and bananas, with the explanation that there was nothing like getting used to the dirt beforehand. Edith Richland carried her to the steamer in her carriage, and there were books and flowers to testify to the kindly feeling of others. "If people really regret my going," said Maud, "I shall be glad to return. I did not know that I had so many friends."

Mr. Delavan himself was there, having come on from the West with his daughter and the Professor's family, determined to see that the expedition started in good order. Mr. Delavan might have stood as a type of the successful capitalist; while his glance was keen and his face seamed with lines indicative of shrewdness, there was a certain comfortable good nature suggested by his kindly smile and the generous outlines of his portly figure. He had brought a bundle of the latest newspapers, damp from the press. "You will be glad enough to

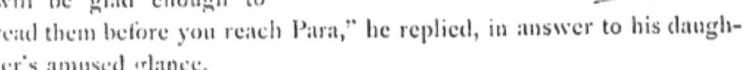

read them before you reach Para," he replied, in answer to his daughter's amused glance.

"But, papa," Victoria protested, "of what possible interest to us are the stock quotations and police news?"

"Ah! just there," Mr. Delavan replied, "is a remarkably juicy bit of information. A Mr. Bartlett, corresponding secretary of the firm of Gold, Glitter & Co., has just absconded with an enormous amount of cash. He had the firm's implicit confidence, and was a genius in his way, being thoroughly conversant with five languages. It is supposed that he sailed for Europe on one of yesterday's steamers; but detectives are on his track, and he will certainly be caught."

"Only to think!" exclaimed Maud, "he may even be on this very steamer. I wonder whether we shall meet him."

"You will find his description in that paper," replied Mr. Delavan, "but very probably he is cleverly disguised."

"Do read it," Delight begged. "There are certain characteristics, as the color of the eyes, which cannot be disguised, and I would like to be able to recognize him."

Victoria took up the despised paper and read: "Mr. Bartlett is a person of medium height, of prepossessing appearance and handsome face, showing the striking combination of light complexion and hair with dark eyes. He dressed his whiskers in the English style, affecting English mannerisms, also, in speech and toilet. He was a good talker, and an accomplished linguist, speaking French, German, Spanish, and Portuguese with equal fluency.

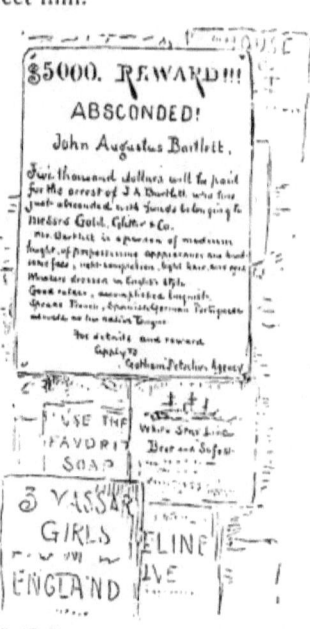

FIVE THOUSAND DOLLARS REWARD.

He had carried on extensive correspondence for the firm with houses in Bordeaux, Marseilles, Hamburg, Bremen, Barcelona, Lisbon, and Oporto, and it is naturally supposed that he will seek refuge in one of these cities. All outgoing steamers are closely watched, and it is the opinion of the detective force that he has not yet left the country. A reward of five thousand dollars is offered for his apprehension."

While they were discussing the matter in the most animated manner, the warning-bell rang all but the tourists on shore. There they stood, making a gay group of fluttering ribbons, scarfs, and curls, with the dark background of the wharf with its bales and boxes. The green Brazilian flag bellied and tugged over the little group on deck, displaying the cross of the Order of Christ and the sphere of the old Portuguese explorers. Maud tore her flowers apart and pelted her friends on shore with Jacqueminot roses. The whole scene was pretty enough for a picture, as an itinerant photographer evidently thought, for he had planted his tripod near the binnacle and was taking instantaneous views by the dozen. Mr. Delavan pushed his way ashore, the last to leave the ship, and as he stepped off, the gang plank was drawn in. The engine gave a convulsive throb, there was a shiver through the entire frame of the steamer, and through the widening space between it and the wharf the shiny water rushed as through a sluice-way; but at that moment a gentleman hurried excitedly through the crowd and leaped on board. The momentum of his spring threw him against the camp-chair upon which Maud was leaning, jostling her slightly. He raised his hat with a polite apology, and then darted down to the cabin. Maud looked up and saw the photographer regarding her with a peculiar expression of interest. "He has just taken your photograph," Victoria whispered, "with that distinguished looking gentleman bowing to you. How disagreeable to have him about; he will be photographing us all when we least suspect it. I wish I had thought to have father forbid his pointing his camera at us."

The steamer had backed into the main stream, had turned and was

BRAZILIAN FLAG.

slipping down the harbor, the round fort on Governor's Island was behind them, the pretty villas gleamed white on Staten Island, a Cunarder just beside them was steaming out to England — Maud might have tossed a ball on board, and how widely they were soon to be separated! A bark which had seen heavy weather was being towed in, and there were darting, puffing tugs, lazy sloops, and all manner of river and sea craft. They remained on deck watching the animated scene until the long line of hotels on Coney Island sunk into the horizon, and a heavy ground swell off Sandy Hook sent them to their state-rooms.

CHAPTER II

THE VOYAGE.

WITH all Maud's experience of travel she was a poor sailor, and for several days sea-sickness held her a prisoner. She could hear the others laughing and chatting in the cabin and on deck, for since they had crossed the Gulf Stream the sea was smooth, but to her, life was a giddy, nauseating chaos, and she realized the opinion of one of William Black's characters, "It is a sickening thing to be sick."

She had hardly strength enough to stretch out her hand to the smelling-salts in her convenient little wall-pocket, or to scowl at the stewardess, who would persist in offering her that wretched beef tea.

But one morning the waves knocked against the side of the vessel in a gentle, sleepy way, the sun shone brightly in upon her, and the air from her open port-hole was fresh and invigorating. Delight came in and helped her to dress, and Maud acknowledged that she might feel better on deck. "Though I never can get there, it is quite impossible," she asserted, closing her eyes with a shudder.

"I will manage it," Delight said, helping her to a seat in a wicker arm-chair just outside the stateroom door, and tucking her in with fleecy wraps. Then she ran away for the steward, and presently there were men's voices, and Maud felt herself lifted and carried upon deck. Here the fresh air revived her, and she was received with merry greetings from the rest of the party. The sailors were heaving the log, and she found herself experiencing a languid interest in the ship's rate of speed. She changed her estimate of Victoria as she noticed how her costume had been modified to suit the exigencies of travel. Miss Delavan now wore a flannel travelling-dress, with a broad alligator-skin belt fastened by curiously wrought silver clasps. She was not a beautiful girl, but there was rare intelligence in the quiet, reserved face, and if there was disdain there, there was also true nobility of character. Maud noticed with satisfaction that the

HEAVING THE LOG.

diamond ear-rings had disappeared. "That is Delight's influence," she said to herself. "One cannot be long in the company of that sensible little puss without following her example."

Victoria was scanning the horizon through a field-glass offered her by a dark-skinned Brazilian. There was something familiar in his attitude, and a second glance told her that he was the polite stranger who had been so tardy in coming on board.

Delight noticed her look of inquiry, and remarked, "That is the Senhor José Ignacio da Silva, a wealthy Brazilian, who is returning to his estates after a visit in the north. He seems to have taken quite a fancy to Victoria, at least. I fancy that she is the attraction, though he is very polite to us all."

Maud's attention was now attracted to a modest appearing young man with whom the Professor had been conversing, and whom he now brought forward and introduced as Dr. Stillman.

MAUD AND THE DOCTOR.

"I shall feel quite secure," Maud remarked, "now that I know we have a physician on board."

"I am rather a student than a practising physician," the young man remarked, in a deprecatory way; "the ink is too fresh on my diploma for me to flourish my M. D. pretentiously."

"And so you are going to South America, to make experiments on the natives?"

"Hardly," he replied, "I still preserve my character of student, my specialty just now being *materia medica*. We are indebted to Brazil, you know, for many of our most powerful drugs, and the object of my journey is to investigate native remedies, and, if possible, add a few new ones to those already known to science."

His manner was so very quiet and unassuming that his intention seemed the most natural and commonplace thing in the world. There was nothing particularly striking about the little doctor; his dress was inconspicuous, his hair an ordinary shade of brown; his eyes could only be guessed at, for they were hidden behind spectacles of London-smoke, but Maud had not the slightest doubt that they were inoffensively gray. For some reason the Professor liked him, probably because he was something of a botanist, and for his gentle, respectful manner, but Maud felt that his presence was rather unnecessary, and hoped that once arrived upon the Amazon he would become so much interested in sarsaparilla and Peruvian bark as to lose sight of their party. Victoria, who joined them soon after, ignored his presence altogether, and if Delight was kind to him, it was only because it was an impossibility for Delight to be rude to any one. Senhor Silva came forward and was introduced; he spoke English without accent, but he was very foreign looking. His hair curled closely to his head in jetty rings, and his complexion was more than sallow, it was almost saffron. When it transpired that Maud had visited Portugal, he chatted pleasantly of Lisbon, which it seemed was his birthplace.

SENHOR SILVA.

"I became slightly acquainted with a family of your name, in Lisbon," Maud remarked; and the Senhor listened with interest while she related a little adventure in the Library of National Archives, how an obliging student had helped them translate the old records of the Inquisition, and how he brought his mother to call upon them; and Senhora Silva, in her turn, extended courtesies.

taking them to the never-to-be-forgotten graduating exercises of her daughter's class at the Convent do Bom Successo.

When Maud had finished her story, Senhor Silva asked, "And did Jesuino or his sister Candida never mention a half-brother in the wilds of Brazil?"

"They spoke of acquaintances there, but I do not remember any brother."

"Ah! that comes from remaining so long from home. I must certainly go to Lisbon next year, and bring them all out to see their myth of a brother."

"Then are you really related?"

"From your description I have no doubt that the Senhora Silva of whom you speak is my step-mother, and Jesuino and Candida my half-brother and sister. Was not the mother rather stout, with dark hair and eyes, and had she not a mole on the left cheek?"

"On the right, I think."

"Precisely. Did they take you out to their quinta at Cintra?"

"No; I do not think they spoke of having one there, and we were at Cintra several days; Jesuino was studying at Coimbra. What a queer old town it is. Did you graduate there?"

"I am sorry to say that I am not a university man. I emigrated to Brazil and was deep in politics when I should have been whisking my student's gown through the college cloisters."

That Senhor Silva was related to her good Portuguese friends was at once a passport, and for the remainder of the voyage he assumed the easy footing of an old acquaintance.

Of their other fellow-passengers Maud only noticed a tonsured priest, reading his breviary, and, pacing the upper deck alone, a senhora from Rio, returning from a visit to the North, and a little governess going out to a family in Pernambuco.

Recovery from sea-sickness is always rapid, and the next day Maud was able to get out her water-colors, and to begin a sketch of

A LEAF FROM MAUD'S SKETCH-BOOK.

the open sea. She was sitting under the shelter of the smoke-stack, at a little distance from her party, to whom Delight was reading aloud from Bates' "Naturalist on the Amazons," when a broad shadow fell across her paper, and the photographer addressed her:

"Excuse the intrusion," he remarked glibly. "I am myself an artist in an humble way; my name is Jenkins and I will be obliged if you will examine some of my work."

As he spoke he offered her a package of photographs, and Maud's artistic impulses conquered the slight aversion which she felt for the pushing character of the individual. She looked over his views, and inquired if they were for sale, for many of them were very good.

"I regret," he replied, "that I have not provided myself with sufficient material to dispose of any

THE PHOTOGRAPHER, MR. JENKINS.

during the voyage; but if you would favor me with an order, I would be happy to send them to your address." He drew out a pencil and note-book ready to jot down the numbers, but Maud replied that she did not particularly care for marines, she was more interested in faces.

"Then you will enjoy looking over this scrap-book," Mr. Jenkins replied, taking one from the inner pocket of his overcoat. "I have here a portrait of every individual on board, from the captain to the cook's assistant."

"How did you induce them all to sit?" Maud asked, incredulously.

"They didn't know they were sitting; I have my little sneak-box," (lifting a canvas-covered box with leather straps, an extremely inoffensive looking travelling-bag), "and I sit with it under my arm until I catch the person I want, then I sight it, so, press this pneumatic tube, and pop! the thing is done."

"You were using an ordinary camera the day we embarked"—

"Yes, I have both, but for unconscious instantaneous pictures there is nothing like my little friend here. See, I have caught the Professor in the midst of a yawn; there's an open countenance for you! and here is the Brazilian lady slyly taking a pinch of snuff behind her lace handkerchief; she has no idea she has gone on record for that little weakness. This sailor with his arm extended is heaving the log. There you are yourself, with that Portugee gentleman bowing to you; he's an uncommonly uneasy sitter; he seems to have eyes in the back of his head; as soon as I get him nicely sighted he turns square round, or wiggles, or tips his hat; but I'll have him yet. That young Doctor, too, is a vexatious specimen; his spectacles are regular reflectors, and throw the light all over his countenance. I wish he could be induced to take them off a minute."

"I will try to help you," Maud made offer impulsively. "I will get each of them to pose for me, and then you will have a good opportunity."

The next morning her offer was forgotten, for they were steaming into the crater-like harbor of St. Thomas, one of the Virgin Islands of the West Indies. All around them on sea and mountain and city, was flung the conflagration of a mid-summer sunrise, such as they had never seen equalled.

"It is like a transformation scene in a fairy ballet," said Senhor Silva. The Professor gave him a look of withering scorn. "Sir," he exclaimed, "it is the New Jerusalem!" Maud was silent, but her eyes were filled with mist. This beauty was so supernatural that it called for tears.

Soon the ship was surrounded by importunate boatmen, anxious to ferry the passengers to the shore. In one boat were little ragged, half-naked blacks, screaming for dimes. Senhor Silva threw some coins overboard, and the shining darkies plunged into the water, struggling with one another, until one victoriously reappeared with a nickel in his mouth; and the diving was repeated as Victoria tossed more small change over the ship's side.

Meanwhile the Doctor had secured a boat and was assisting the party into it. They were to have but a stay of six hours and he was eager to show them the picturesque city. Senhor Silva recommended the place for the cheapness of its bay-rum and cigars, and pointed out the island of Santa Cruz from which the rum was brought, some forty miles away. The Doctor was more interested in the history of the city, and showed them old buildings dating back to the time of the Danes, and unrepaired ruins from the hurricane and great tidal wave of a dozen years previous. Maud watched with admiration the swarthy blacks coaling the vessel, women aiding in the work gayly attired, and the proud swing of their powerful bodies suggesting poses for her sketch-book.

DIVING FOR COINS.

Victoria entered a small curiosity shop and invested in souvenirs, a set of pearly fish-scale jewelry for Delight, some rare shells for the Professor, and some barbaric handkerchiefs as draperies for Maud.

As they returned to the vessel they found themselves in company with Mr. Jenkins, who had been securing negatives of West Indian life. The girls spoke of him as they were arranging their hair for dinner in the dressing-room and Maud related her encounter with him the day previous. Victoria paused in the act of adjusting a Cape jessamine and exclaimed, "Maud Van Vechten, don't you see, he is the detective."

"How clever you are," Maud replied, slowly, "I do believe you are right, and he suspects Senhor Silva and the Doctor."

"Not Senhor Silva," Victoria replied with decision. "How could that be when he has lived all his life in Portugal and Brazil? But the Doctor, that is another matter, and I confess, that, as I study the case, there are suspicious circumstances. I would like to examine his eyes."

BIRTHPLACE OF JOSEPHINE.

Delight laughed merrily. "Victoria talks as if she were a physician looking for symptoms of a disease. I declare, dear, you would make a good doctor; you see right to the causes of everything."

"I a doctor," sneered Victoria; "the very idea! catch me wasting my life in that way."

"What is it to waste life?" Delight questioned, meekly, but Victoria was too deeply absorbed in her new train of thought to mark the query. "We must manage to make him show us his eyes," she repeated, "his hair is probably dyed, it has just that look. How can we abolish the spectacles?"

The opportunity was nearer than they thought.

After the stop at St. Thomas came a delightful sail amongst islands; some small and barren, others, like Guadeloupe, Martinique, and the Barbadoes, covered with tropical foliage, or shooting to the height of five thousand feet, their mountain summits hidden in the clouds.

In speaking of Martinique and of the Empress Josephine's girlhood here Dr. Stillman grew quite enthusiastic, and in his unconscious emotion he removed his spectacles and wiped them carefully, turning his calm glance full upon the three girls. Delight blushed and looked away uneasily, Maud started with a half gasp, but Victoria's keen eyes glittered and she met his wild gaze unflinchingly,— his eyes were uncommonly handsome, and blue-black in their dark melancholy. For an instant there was a hush and then Maud heard a sharp click behind her and knew that Mr. Jenkins had secured his photograph.

THE PROFESSOR FISHING FOR SEA-WEED.

Now came glorious moonlight nights. Every evening showed the pole-star nearer the horizon, until finally it set altogether, and the constellation of the Southern Cross came in sight. They hung over the ship's side, watching the glowing phosphorescent light upon the waters, the Professor always interested in fishing for sea-weed and the beautiful medusæ or jelly fish, and Senhor Silva occasionally shooting at the sharks which followed the vessel. Sometimes they sang. Victoria had a ringing soprano, Delight a rather weak alto,

Senhor Silva a fine tenor, and the Doctor a full, rich bass voice, and many a favorite song was sung in quartette or duo, while the waves lapped the side of the vessel and the moonlight flooded them with its glamor.

"I do not believe," Delight had said to Victoria, "that the Doctor can be the defaulter. It does not seem possible to me that a bad man could sing in such a whole-souled glorious way."

"Ah! little Delight," Victoria had replied, "have you never heard it stated that music has nothing to do with morals?"

"Crossing the line," furnished the occasion for much sport, and many rough practical jokes among the sailors. One old salt was dressed as Neptune, another as his wife, and the afternoon was given up to rollicking carnival, while a new seaman had his head shaved in no very gentle manner. The equator passed, they noticed long before they were in sight of shore the vast volume of turbid fresh water flowing out on the surface of the salt, since its specific gravity is less, and mixing slowly with it. It was the mighty Amazon continuing its course in the ocean after it escaped its banks. The Professor's line brought up tangled bits of foliage, withered and torn fragments of palm leaves.

"If we could descend to the ocean floor in a diving-bell," said the Professor, "we should see the debris of the river channel, sandstone and shale, cut away and brought down from the heart of the continent with deposits of vegetation, building itself gradually into a sub-marine mountain range."

While the Professor was speaking, Senhor Silva swept the horizon with his powerful field-glass. "The lightship is in sight," he said. "We are nearing Para, and there I must bid you farewell for a time, for I have business to transact relative to the purchase of a small cargo steamboat to ply between my sawmills on the upper Amazon and Para. I intend to launch extensively into the exportation of costly woods for cabinet manufacture."

"What are some of the woods to be found on the river?" Maud asked. "I remember seeing some beautiful cabinets in Lisbon formed of a marquetry of precious timbers brought from Brazil in the time of the first explorers, but I hardly fancy I could have told the names of any with the exception of ebony and mahogany."

"Many of the varieties have no English names," Senhor Silva replied. "The different species of *Jacaranda* or rosewood head the list, then comes Palisander, corrupted from Paolo Santo, a violet-tinted wood, the *Moiracoatidra* or zebra wood, the pao d'arco, a rich brown, the tortoise-shell wood, and the *tuya*, intricately mottled, many kinds of cedar and laurels, with others of beautiful graining or marking, capable of a high polish. Dye-woods will also fall in my way, with others of a medicinal character, but I am principally interested in cabinet timbers, and have made a partnership arrangement with a New York firm who will make it their business to introduce them into the United States."

MAUD AND SENHOR SILVA PASSING THE LIGHT-SHIP.

"No country," Maud replied, "is paying more attention to building at present. They will certainly be in demand for mosaic floors, wainscots, and interior finishings."

"When Papa builds the house which he has always promised to give me, I shall order all the wood-work from you," said Victoria.

Senhor Silva bowed. "I will give you an opportunity of selecting and marking the logs, for the Professor has kindly consented to visit my fazenda. We will make an excursion into the forest and you shall yourself blaze the trees which you would like. I will find you before you leave the city and will certainly arrange to make the trip up the river with you. I am sorry that my engagements make it impossible for me to do the honors of Para."

"It will not be necessary," the Professor hastened to assure him. "I am familiar with the city, and Dr. Stillman has kindly agreed to remain with us."

Mr. Jenkins was standing so near, with his neck outstretched with such an expression of interest as the Professor made this remark, that the latter turned and asked the photographer if he wished to speak with him. Not at all disconcerted, Mr. Jenkins asked the hotel at which the party proposed to stop, as he had some photographs to deliver to one of the young ladies.

"The Hotel do Commercio," the Professor replied.

"Thank you," said Mr. Jenkins glibly, "it is very possible that you may see me again."

Senhor Silva turned on his heel with an expression of disgust.

CHAPTER III.

PARA.

HE Para River is the southern mouth of the Amazons, which, as it empties into the Atlantic, separates, seemingly to form a delta, the great island of Marajo, a tract of land as large as the state of New York. But Marajo has not been built up by the river; it has, on the contrary, opposed its rocky foundations to its current, and forced it to either side. The southern channel is the one more easily navigable, and eighty miles from its mouth has been built up the city of Para, which may one day become the metropolis of Brazil. For although Rio Janeiro now surpasses it, Para has the advantage of situation, being nearer the ports of Europe and North America, and with water communication stretching back across the continent.

As they sailed into the harbor, past the little fort, the girls scanned the shore with interest, pointing out the palm-trees, and the white houses nestling in the green of the plantations, with tall crosses marking the tiny chapels by the shore. It was early morning when the party stepped from the launch and were surrounded by porters eagerly demanding their baggage. Dr. Stillman, noticing the Professor's glance of mild wonder at changes which attracted his attention, sprang to the front and led them to the picturesque old custom-house. Here their baggage was examined in a court resembling a cloister-garden in its wealth of graceful, large-leaved plants.

From the custom-house they passed to the Hotel do Commercio. "Ah! this is ghastly," Victoria exclaimed, opening a tiny silver vinaigrette as the sickening odors from a covered drain met them at the doorway.

"They are the spirits of fever and malaria," said the Doctor, "that we shall meet more than once on our journey up the river."

The Professor led the way up the ancient wooden staircase to the balconies overlooking the courtyard. Here parrots screamed and a monkey tugged at his chain. The Doctor pointed to the vultures soaring high in air, with the remark that they were the health commission of Para. "But for these scavengers," he asserted, "the Paranese would bury themselves in garbage."

A white-aproned mulatto now ushered them into the breakfast-room temptingly set with clean cloths and white dishes. "Ah! this is

ASCENDING THE PARA RIVER.

Paradise after Purgatory," Maud exclaimed, pointing to the long windows reaching to the floor with their charming views of the river harbor and shipping. The Hotel boasted a French cook and the bill of fare was not remarkable for oddities.

Maud found the fried bananas delicious. Victoria ordering *Queijo Flamengo* with the idea that it was some preparation of flamingo, was somewhat chagrined at receiving some Holland cheese. The Doctor told of the experience of Lieut. Gibbon, who was asked if he was fond of "*wawas*," the pet name for baby, and mistaking the word for *guavas*, replied that they were much better when preserved than when eaten raw. A burst of laughter greeted his assertion, and he was asked if he had ever eaten one. "Hundreds," he replied, "and I will take one now with the greatest of pleasure."

Mrs. Holmes was seen to examine her bill of fare with something like consternation. "What is it my dear?" asked her husband.

"We certainly ought not to stop at such an expensive place," she replied, "they charge one thousand five hundred reis for breakfast!"

"But a thousand reis is only fifty cents," explained the Professor, "and seventy-five cents is not an exorbitant sum."

After breakfast the Doctor invited the ladies to a drive in an open barouche — the Professor finding himself too much occupied to accompany them. The light was so dazzling that they lifted their sunshades, but the temperature was delightful. They drove along the Rua dos Mercadores or principal business street. Mule-cars ran through the centre and there was more of bustling activity than Maud had expected to find in a tropical city. "The morning is the fashionable hour for the promenade," the Doctor explained. The shops were of various colors and covered with gaudy advertisements, while the display of goods added to the vivid decorative effect, and gave the street the appearance of being draped with pennons and flags. They visited the market, with its piles of pineapples, mangoes, plantains, and oranges, and Maud found here the same splendid negro types which had struck her in Morocco, women with their heads bound with gay 'kerchiefs, or with mops of bushy hair, their white waists slipping off their glossy black shoulders, and their laps filled with some rich-tinted fruit.

"We must patronize the Assai stands," said Mrs. Holmes. "The Professor has often praised this national drink of Brazil."

"What is Assai?" asked Victoria.

"It is the name of a palm," replied Delight, "from whose fruit a kind of sherbet is made, which is said to be very refreshing."

The doctor pointed to some baskets filled with a dark plum-like fruit, and showed them the process by which the pulp was rubbed through sieves into jars of water. The beverage was served to them in small bowls formed of calabashes. Fastidious Victoria hardly sipped hers, but the rest of the party were of the opinion that one might become very fond of it.

"Mrs. Agassiz speaks of it, you remember," said Delight. "She gives the native proverb, and translates it freely for us,—

THE ASSAI STAND.

'Quem vein para Pará parou;
Quem beben Assai ficou:'

Which is, being interpreted,—

'Who came to Pará was glad to stay;
Who drank Assai went never away.'"

From the market they drove to the Botanical Garden, where Victoria, ordinarily undemonstrative, lost her heart to the palms.

"Why don't you make them your specialty, this summer," Delight asked. "You will have a grand opportunity for studying them, and there are at least two hundred different varieties in South America."

"I will study them," Victoria replied; "but only as an amateur, for the love of them. I never could be a specialist, as you understand the term. I want to roam all about this great tangled garden of the world and study just what I like, because it amuses me, and not because it is going to be of any special use to any one else."

The Doctor regarded her with a respectful pity, at least it seemed to Maud that both of these conflicting emotions were mingled in his glance. "It seems to me," he said, "that the keenest amusement is found in things that are of the most use, and in studying the nicety with which nature adapts them to our needs. Take, for instance, a discovery recently made in this very country. A patient of the great French opthalmologist, Dr. Wecker, had been treated for *Pannus*, a disease of the eye, and had only been partially cured. While travelling in Brazil the malady came on again, and he was told of the *Jequerilly* bean, which the Indians used in a decoction for similar trouble. He tried it, was completely cured, and sent some of the beans in a letter to Dr. Wecker, who

TROPICAL PLANTS.

also experimented with them, and announced the discovery of an entirely new remedy. It has already been accepted by science, and can be obtained at almost every pharmacy anywhere in the civilized world.

These beans are of a bright scarlet color, and are perforated by the natives and worn as ornaments. The Indian girl we met at the entrance to the garden had on a necklace of them."

"Why, they were black-eyed Susans," Delight exclaimed. "I have a cup of them at home that an old sea-captain brought from the West Indies."

"The botanical name is *Arbor Precatorius*, so called because they were used for the beads of rosaries."

"Then if any Indian had trouble with his eyes," Maud remarked, "all he had to do was to stew his beads, and anoint his eyes with the holy water. If he were devout, he might ascribe the cure to the efficacy of his amulet."

INDIAN GIRL.

"Very likely, for the Indians are very superstitious; but they have drugs of their own which work in quite as magical a way. Have you ever heard of the *curare*, 'the liquor which kills with a whisper'? It is made of the juices of various plants and attacks the nerves of motion, the heart last of all, so that the victim is to all appearance dead long before life is extinct. He can hear but cannot speak, is conscious of what is passing around him but can make no sign. No antidote is known for this terrible poison."

The Doctor's enthusiasm once excited he passed from one plant to another explaining its properties, or any curious facts concerning its growth or history. Victoria listened with a well-bred assumption of interest, but she told her companions afterward that she was inwardly raging. "The idea," she exclaimed, "of his forcing upon us a lecture about his old drugs when all I wanted was to enjoy those exquisite flowers."

He atoned for the infliction, however, for he drove them home by way of the Estrada de Sao José, and here, as Victoria acknowledged, she first saw palms. These were royal palms imported from Mauritius among the most beautiful of the entire family. One looked down a colonnade of stately columns crowned with a mass of feathery foliage, shifting, whispering with the slightest motion of the air, while the mast-like trunks are said to remain perfectly unmoved even in storms.

They were outside the city when they passed an Indian woman seated by the side of the road in an attitude of extreme dejection, a bundle of rags lay at a little distance, under the shadow of a mango tree, and from the bundle a hand waved with an action expressive of the utmost misery.

CARRYING THE SICK CHILD.

The Doctor stopped the carriage, and leaping down from his seat beside the driver, hurried back to the forlorn objects. Presently he approached and motioned them to go on to the city. Looking back they saw that the woman had risen and that she and the Doctor were supporting the sick child between them in a small hammock. "They are taking it to the hospital," the driver explained. "It is probably a leper."

It was sultry noon by the time they returned to the hotel. "I have been quite anxious about you," said the Professor. "It is time you were taking your siestas. You will have sunstroke if you run about at such unnatural hours."

"Maud," Delight called sleepily from her hammock, just as her friend was dropping into a dream, "does this remind you at all of your visit to Morocco?"

"No, dear, it is very different. That was an old, old civilization crumbling to dust; this is a new world just born."

"You haven't reached the newness yet. We will find that up the river. Are you not wild to begin your sketching?"

"If you will come down by the river-side with me this afternoon we will see what we can find among the Indian types."

Silence succeeded for a few moments, unbroken except by the sleepy creak of the hammock ropes, and then Delight spoke again, "Victoria, what book have you there? I verily believe you are reading."

"They are some manuscript papers of Dr. Stillman's on Indian poisons, and they are intensely interesting."

"I thought you did not care for his old drugs."

"Well I don't sympathize with his thirst for beneficence, the discovery of new remedies, and all that; but I always had a liking for chemistry. If I had lived in the dark ages I would have been an alchemist or a Lucretia Borgia, just for the fascination of seeing the fluids work."

"Victoria," said Maud. "I believe you will turn out a genius if you only will work."

"That is precisely what I will not do," Victoria replied.

"O Victoria," Delight objected, "you do work when you are interested in a thing. You should have seen her last year at College,

Maud. The scheme for this trip became what the French call an *idée fixée* with her and she made all her studies tend towards it. She was like the young man that Hamerton tells about, who was preparing to be an explorer and who used to upset himself in the lake, and besides swimming and riding and shooting, learned carpentry and sewing and cooking and all sorts of wood-craft to prepare himself for a wild life. Victoria took private lessons in taxidermy, so as to be prepared to mount specimens, and the other accomplishments of the young explorer, with the exception of carpentry, she mastered at home."

"I should think you would have found taxidermy very disagreeable," Maud remarked.

"I did at first," Victoria replied, "but I came to understand how one can become an enthusiastic surgeon even. By the bye I have changed my opinion in regard to Dr. Stillman. After seeing him help that poor woman with the sick child I am certain that he is no defaulter; he is only an innocent fanatic."

The afternoon was cool and pleasant. The dazzling light shimmered now in long slant beams instead of splintering its lances from the zenith, and the girls sallied out together for a stroll along the *Rua da Imperatriz* to the water side. The wholesale stores were closed, for this was the hour when the well-to-do merchants left business to sit in their gardens sipping coffee and smoking cigarettes with guests who sauntered in for an afternoon chat. Along the shore canoes were drawn up, and under the awnings or *toldas*, the girls could see the shy brown faces of the Indian women, or the bold black ones of negresses. They had come, many of them, from long distances to market their wares at Para; gaudily decorated pottery, calabashes, Brazil nuts, fish and cacao. Maud was attracted to one boat gay with macaws and paroquets which a little naked child was feeding. A jaguar-skin hung over the side of the boat, and a palm branch drooped from the awning.

Altogether it was an uncommonly picturesque combination, and Maud, delighted, shook out her camp-stool, and unjointed her easel. Delight threw a shawl on the ground, and spreading the great white sketching umbrella, seated herself by Maud's side, prepared to read aloud from Southey's History of Brazil. The Indian woman came to meet them, her hands filled with bows and arrows, and actuated quite as much by curiosity as by a desire to sell the articles.

Victoria examined her wares. "These arrows are poisoned," she said; and she repeated the word "*curare?*" in a questioning way. The woman understood her and nodded, talking volubly in the *lingua geral*, or *Tupi* dialect.

"Will you see if she understands Portuguese?" Victoria asked of Maud. It seemed that she did understand, for she replied to Maud's questions, that the poison was manufactured by an Indian witch, who lived far up the river, in the neighborhood of Obidos.

"I wonder whether the witch can manufacture medicines as well as poisons," Victoria mused; "if so, Dr. Stillman ought to have her address."

Maud carried on the conversation a little further, eliciting the information that the witch had a famous remedy for the *tertiana*, a malarial fever, and that her name was Justimiama dos Reis.

Victoria made a careful note of this, as she declared for Dr. Stillman's benefit, and she bought two of the arrows, which tipped, as they were with toucan feathers, were very decorative objects. A party of jauntily dressed *Mamelucos*, or half-breed herdsmen, strolling that way, alarmed the girls soon after, and they returned to the hotel before Maud had finished her sketch.

The next day was the Sabbath, the fete-day of Saint Somebody, and as there were to be great ceremonies at Nazareth, the party took the mule-car for the suburb. Nossa Senhora de Nazareth, in her spangled gauze dress, reminded Maud of some of the Spanish images of the Virgin.

Every day was made hideous at certain hours by the clangorous ringing of bells, which was managed in an altogether unique way. Boys mount into the belfries and beat lustily upon the bells with hammers. As the girls approached the church they could see them maintaining their vigorous anvil exercise, delighting in the discord which they produced with all the barbarous love of ear-rending noise which our northern boys indulge in on the eve of the glorious Fourth.

The ceremonies were rather tawdry than imposing, the only startling feature being the sending up of rockets by the devotees which were supposed to be the carriers of prayers to heaven. The cemetery seemed to be the favorite spot for religious pyrotechnics. Maud wondered whether the idea was borrowed from the Chinese, and Victoria suggested that it might have been handed down from the fire-worshippers.

ROCKET PRAYERS.

On Monday the Professor manifested some impatience to start up the river, but Delight pleaded for a longer visit at Para. "We have not begun to explore its beauties," she argued; "and you ought to give Maud a chance to make some sketches for herself, for very soon you will keep her busy drawing hideous fossil fish. Besides, had they not told Senhor Silva that they would leave on the Saturday boat, and was it fair not to keep their appointment?"

The last consideration prevailed, and the Doctor took them again for an excursion to the outskirts.

They started at earliest dawn and drove out of the city before it had fully awakened, only here and there a servant was yawning sleepily as she stared at them from behind the Venetian blinds. As they left the streets and struck the broad Una road the sun rose and a flood of light was poured over the fresh leaves. Large shield-shaped arums, vines and trees mixed in one inextricable tangle. Strange flowers starred the thickets; everything was new and tropical and interesting. They caught glimpses of picturesque *rocinhas*, or country houses, with tiled roofs, and walls a mass of vines, and they came out upon the banks of the lovely Una river, palm-shaded, with drifts of butterflies fluttering over its placid surface.

"It is all delicious," Maud exclaimed, "but it makes me wild to think how little of this beauty I can carry away."

"Take it away in your soul, child," exclaimed Victoria.

"And so I shall," replied Maud, "but it seems selfish to enjoy all this and do nothing to make others enjoy it too."

"I wonder we don't come across our friend the photographer spotting some of this beautiful scenery," the Doctor remarked.

"Mr. Jenkins was more interested in human types," Delight replied. "I do not think we shall meet him again."

Oddly enough they came across him that very evening. The girls were paying a visit to the shop of Monkey Joe, an animal store. "What a menagerie it is!" Maud exclaimed. "Here are snakes and armadillos, monkeys and wild hogs, electric eels, and every variety of queer bird; here is even — " and just then, from the outer yard, where the larger wild beasts were kept, Mr. Jenkins appeared with his sneak-box.

"Have you been photographing the animals?" Delight asked.

"No miss," he replied, "but the people who come to see them. Monkey Joe's is the most attractive spot in Para. Sooner or later, all strangers come here; but I haven't yet succeeded in shooting the party I am in search of."

"Dear me, I hope you don't mean to assassinate any one!" Maud exclaimed.

Mr. Jenkins laughed, and asked when they expected to start up the river.

Victoria had no intention that he should be informed, and drew Maud away, with an exclamation of enthusiasm for a strangely human little monkey who was looking at them appealingly from his wistful black eyes. It is a Coata, Joe says, and has long black hair, a match, Victoria thinks, for her winter furs. Indeed if it were not for those expressive eyes peering out from under the silky bang, the monkey might be mistaken for a muff.

The little thing came shyly down from its perch and licked Victoria's fingers, and she was further interested in it by the information that it was an orphan and had sulked since its mother died, refusing to eat, though it now accepted the food which Victoria offered it.

Several days of great heat succeeded, when none of the party cared to remain long upon the streets, and they realized why Brazil was named from the Portuguese word *braza*, burning embers. "We certainly are in a brazier," Maud announces, "and the sooner we set out upon our river trip the better."

"Perhaps we will find that it is only out of the frying pan into the fire," Victoria suggests languidly; but she has hardly force to object, nor does she care to do so, now that the time agreed upon with Senhor Silva has arrived. It is rather strange that they have neither heard nor seen anything of him in Para. Granted that he was too busy to call, he might at least have sent them some token of remembrance; but Victoria is sure that he will keep his appointment with them; and they leave on the midnight boat, the stars shining clear overhead and a refreshing breeze striking them as they steam out into the Marajo Bay.

Half of the upper deck, back of the smoke-stacks, is assigned to their party, and here they fasten their hammocks under the awning. They scan the half dozen first-class passengers as they come on board; but the boat is off and away and the Senhor is not among them.

Victoria wraps herself in her travelling shawl, and retires to her hammock, taciturn, and even ill-humored. She purposely neglects to bid the Doctor good-night, as if he were in any way to blame for her disappointment.

CHAPTER IV.

A PALMER'S PILGRIMAGE.

"IT certainly seems like Sunday," said Delight, the next day after several hours of silent voyaging; for the different members of the expedition were all too much interested in the moving panorama of the shore to chat much.

"It is Palm Sunday, then," said Victoria, "for see how they spring up everywhere, over-topping the other foliage, and breaking into fountains and waves of plumy green spray."

"Yes, the palms hold revel here," said the Professor. "I can count a dozen varieties in a half hour's sail — feathery *Jupatis* drooping over the river side, giant *Miritis*, like the columns of some temple, graceful *Assais*, shooting up into the air, true rocket trees, and *Bussus*, with their elegant wine-glass outlines. As Professor Agassiz says, the remarkable common character which palms possess as a class does not prevent the most striking difference between various kinds. He goes on to class them by the different arrangement of their leaves, the *Baccabas* being disposed in pairs one above another, the *Inajas* in cycles of five spread slightly, so as to form an open vase, the *Assai* has an eight-leaved arrangement, the *Cocoanut palm* disposes its leaves in groups of thirteen, and so on."

"Mrs. Agassiz describes the fruitage of the palms with the eye of a true artist," Maud remarked. "Only note the sense of color in this paragraph:

"'The *Baccaba*, or wine-palm, from which the flowers droop in long crimson cords, with bright green berries from distance to distance along their length, like an immense coral tassel flecked here and there with green, hanging from the dark trunk of the tree. On the *Cocoanut* palm the flowers burst from the sheath in such a long plume of soft creamy white blossoms; such a plume is so heavy with the weight of pendent blossoms that it can hardly be lifted, and its effect is very striking, hanging high up on the trunk just under the green vault of leaves.'"

"The palm is the providence of the natives of South America," said the Professor; "it serves them for raiment, shelter, food, drink, fuel, cordage for hammocks, nets and fishing-tackle, its wax for candles, and its oil for illuminating purposes, while beautifying the landscape with their graceful forms."

"What a delightful Palmer's pilgrimage it would be," mused the Doctor, "to follow the palm around the globe, through all the countries to which it is a native, — to find the date palm in the oases of Africa, to note its sister varieties shading the ruins of ancient Egypt, to walk through Palmyra, the city of palms, and Elim, where were forty palm trees; to find it again in Persia, in the hanging gardens of Babylon, in India, and, in short, in all of the fascinating lands of the Orient."

"That is almost too extensive a tour even for my imagination," replied Victoria. "How many varieties of palms are there, Professor?"

THE TEMPLE OF ISIS.

"About five hundred are known. The most complete treatise on the subject is the monograph by Martius, a large work containing over two hundred colored plates; but it was written in the early half of this century, and many new species have been discovered. I recommend you to begin a monograph of your own."

"There would be a certain fitness in your taking up the study of palms," said the Doctor, "for you remember that the early signification of the palm-branch was victory, and your name is Victoria."

"But I do not deserve it," Victoria replied. "I remember reading a poem in a magazine long ago; only one verse remains with me:

> "'O fainting soul that readest well this story,
> Longing through pain for death's benignant balm,
> Think not to win a heaven of rest and glory
> If thou shalt reach its gates without thy palm.'"

It was so unusual for Victoria to express a sentiment like this, that all were silent for a moment. It was her own voice that broke the stillness with some merry remark on quite another subject.

Their life on board the river-steamer was quite a family one. The shore side of the upper deck was given up to their use, and the long table, on which not over-tempting meals were served them, was strewn between mealtime with books, writing and drawing materials, specimens, and the working paraphernalia of a naturalist. Delight was busy classifying and fitting in her herbarium the ferns which she had collected in the vicinity of Para. Maud sketched constantly. Mrs. Holmes busied herself with some light needlework. The Professor was continually taking notes, examining the fish which were prepared for the table, making observations with meteorological instruments, or flitting to different parts of the boat to make inquiries on every imaginable subject. Only the Doctor and Victoria were idle, and, seated in reclining chairs, chatted while the lovely landscape glided by. It was the Doctor who talked most; Victoria only listened.

Maud noticed that the Doctor conversed generally upon the subject in which he was most interested, and that Victoria in spite of herself was entertained. She asked questions, and read the books which he lent her, dry, technical books, she would have called them a short time before. Maud was indiscreet enough to say to Victoria, at one time when they found themselves alone together, that she thought the Doctor had a very good influence over her.

Victoria flushed indignantly. "You are greatly mistaken," she replied, " he has not the slightest influence whatever."

" I beg your pardon," Maud said, coolly touching in a bit of cloud with a critical air, " then the improvement may possibly be Delight's influence."

" What improvement do you mean?" Victoria asked in a resentful way.

" I refer to your sudden interest in botany, and your wakening from your old listlessness."

" Have I not a right to be listless if I choose?"

" No, I think not, 'to whom much is given, of him, you know, much shall be required.' "

" Yes; but if I make the Professor and Delight my substitutes,— if I give them the opportunity of doing more than I ever could personally,— I should think my responsibility might end."

" I fear I have offended you," Maud said more kindly, as she saw that the girl was really in earnest, "but Victoria, I do not think any of us can be excused from personal service in this warfare. Your money is being put to a noble use, but the world has a claim on your talent as well."

" I have no talent," Victoria replied, shortly.

" If you are sure of that you have an excuse for inaction; but be sure you do not send in false returns of this kind of property to the tax-collector."

Delight suddenly appeared at this juncture with the news that they had been signalled from the shore, and that a boat was approaching. They could see a man waving his handkerchief,—some would-be passenger, who wished to be taken on board. Maud eyed the figure intently, confident that their missing friend had at last kept his appointment, and Victoria took more than one long look through the field-glass before she could convince herself that this was not Senhor Silva, but as the boat neared the steamer a simultaneous exclamation of recognition burst from the party. It was Mr. Jenkins.

The Doctor seemed, if possible, more annoyed to meet him than the others, and all felt his coming an intrusion. He did not, however, appear at first inclined to trouble them with his society, but greeting each member of the party with a familiar nod, he retired with his camera to the rear of the steamboat.

They were nearing Breves, where they were to land. Here they made their first acquaintance with the rubber industry. As the boat was

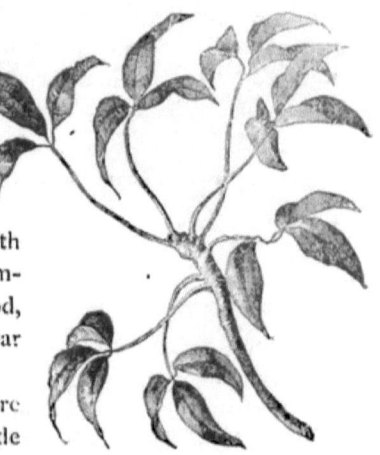

SIPHONIA ELASTICA.

to make quite a stop, an excursion was planned in canoes to the rubber swamps. Mrs. Holmes was sure that the place was infested with malaria and mosquitos, and did not care to go. There was room for three beside the Indian boatman in each canoe. The Professor, Victoria, and the Doctor took their places in the first. Maud and Delight were seated in the second, and the canoe-man was just about to push away, when Mr. Jenkins hurried up with his sneak-box and begged to be included in the party. They could not refuse, and the two boats shot from the shore away under interlacing boughs into the dusk and silence of the forest. Palms, lianas, and a dense underbrush were all matted and tangled together on every side. Their guide pointed out the rubber trees, the *Siphonia Elastica*, and they noticed the gashes cut in the bark, and the little clay cups set to collect the milky sap.

They were paddled across the swamp, to the hut of a rubber-collector, or *seringuerio*. He was bent with ague and rheumatism, and his poor home was built on stilt-like supports, to raise it above flood-level. The palm-thatched roof projected like that of a Swiss chalet, over balconies where hammocks were hung for the siesta; at night they were carried into the interior, and the door, — there was no window, — was closed to keep out the mosquitos. All around them was the forest, so dense that it was impossible to penetrate it to any distance except by the path made by the rubber-collector, who spends his days wading through marshy grounds where lurk poisonous water-snakes, and jungles where jaguars prowl.

The gatherer, as he goes his daily rounds, makes a number of fresh cuts around the trunk of each tree, sets his cups, and passes on. Later in the day he makes the same rounds, with a queer pail manufactured from a calabash, with a braided cover and handle, into which he empties the sap collected in the little cups, which in turn he pours into the shell of a great *torturuga* or turtle. The Professor explained the process after this. Delight noticed a tall earthen jar which she examined curiously, for she could not imagine for what use it was intended. "What do you think it is?" asked the Professor.

"It looks like a lamp chimney," Delight replied, "though it is much too large."

"It is a chimney, however," replied the Professor, "a fire of palm nuts is made beneath it, and the rubber is prepared by dipping the blade of this long wooden paddle into the rubber sap, and then coagulating the fluids by holding the paddle in the dense white smoke, which pours from the top of the chimney."

The seringuerio obligingly went through the operation. The

A KUBBER SETTLEMENT.

smoke hardened the sap into a leathery substance, and at the same time changed it to a yellow color. As fast as it hardened, the man poured on more sap, until quite a mass of rubber had collected on the paddle, when he sliced off the cake of rubber with a knife. Each of the girls made a cake of her own, and speculated as to the use to which it might finally be put. "I have no doubt," said Victoria, "that mine will go to Europe; will be vulcanized and manipulated in various ways, and finally made up into a set of rubber jewelry."

"I should prefer that mine should be put to some useful purpose," said Delight, "spread thin over a gossamer water-proof; or made into a rubber doll for some baby girl."

"I will take mine in its crude state," said Maud, "and use it just as it is in the service of Art for erasing faulty pencil marks."

"I remember," said Delight, "seeing a rubber-tree in a green-house, when I was a small child, and that the gardener, a whimsical man, told me that its fruit was cut into over-shoes, and that children's sizes were picked before they had ripened."

"That is no more absurd than some of the notions ignorant people form," said the Doctor. "In the early part of this century there was a great furore in England for exporting all kinds of manufactures to Brazil. Some enterprising man sent a cargo of warming-pans, blankets, and skates, articles for which one would think little demand could be found in the tropics; but his wares found a good market, for the planters used the warming-pans for sugar ladles; the blankets as strainers in the gold regions; and the skates were fastened to boxes for rockers in the diamond washing districts."

"That reminds me," said Mr. Jenkins, "of a trader on the Amazons, who imported a quantity of playing cards, but could not sell them because the Indians were not educated up to California Jack. But the man was not to be outwitted; he gave each of the face cards a different name, and sold them for fifty cents a piece, as portraits of the Saints. Fancy the King of Hearts as St. Francis Xavier!"

"It would do better as a representation of Joseph in his coat of many colors," Maud remarked drily. The photographer gave her a look of gratitude, for the Doctor evidently avoided him. He now posed his camera and took in rapid succession several fine negatives of the forest, with its broad-leaved arums growing lush and rank by the water-side against a dark background of dense, tangled vegetation.

AFTER A LIZARD.

"The rubber-tree," exclaimed the Professor, "is a giant species of milk-weed;" and then he sprang ankle deep into the swamp after a rare lizard that was basking on the trunk of a tree.

"This is an excellent place to begin your study of palms," said the doctor to Victoria. "There are five varieties beside that spring; can you tell me their names?"

Maud was working rapidly, her sketch box open on her lap; while Delight brushed away the mosquitos which were singing in the dusk.

MANUFACTURE OF RUBBER.

"I understand now," she said to Maud, "why the house has no windows. He closes the door at night, and kindles a little smoky fire inside, to keep out those horrible insects. Mother was quite right not to come. Do you remember how Jules Verne classifies the different species; 'the gray, the hairy, the white-clawed, the dwarf, the trumpeter, the little fifer, the harlequin, the big black, and the red of the woods?'"

"I am not a microscopist," Maud replied, "but I think I could make a better classification than that. In my limited experience I have already observed at least eighteen varieties; viz: the giant, the nightmare, the always voracious, the ogre, the contralto, the soprano, the alto, the tenor, the basso, the chorus, the violoncello, the first violin, the trombone, the harp, the cornet, the flute, the zithern, the triangle, and indeed the whole orchestra, with all the names ever given to all the hobgoblins."

MAUD'S SKETCH IN THE RUBBER SWAMP.

"There is a difference in their notes." Delight assented musingly, "some are thin and high, and others full and rich. We have had educated fleas on exhibition in New York. I wonder how it would do to give mosquito symphony concerts."

"Our time is half up," announced the Doctor, "we must paddle away, if we are to secure any of that gaudy painted pottery for which Breves is noted."

The Professor's canoe led the way through the *ygapo*, or forest swamp, past cane brakes, over which rosy spoon-bills fluttered, and where alligators slipped now and then with a heavy thud into the water, through a labyrinth of small lakes and channels called *iga-*

rapés or canoe paths, along which great, blue butterflies, whose wings have a wonderful metallic lustre, skim lazily, and the mangroves stoop to the clear water. The Doctor, the Professor, and Victoria, are out of hearing, when Mr. Jenkins startles the two girls with him by a strange question:

"Miss Van Vechten, did I understand you to say that you were acquainted with the family of the Senhor Silva, who was our companion on the steamer?"

"I knew his mother, brother, and sister, in Lisbon. Will you tell me why you ask?"

MR. JENKINS TAKES THE GIRLS INTO CONFIDENCE.

"Yes, if you two young ladies can keep it to yourselves. I am a detective, sent out from New York by Gold, Glitter & Co., to trace the confidential clerk who levanted with so much of their cash. From information which I received at Para, and from my own personal observation on board the steamer, I am positive that the rascal is one of two men."

Maud and Delight looked at each other in suspense.

"Either he is Senhor Silva, or else he is this precious doctor that the Professor has taken such a fancy to."

"O no!" exclaimed Delight; "my father could not be so deceived!"

"He is a perfect gentleman," said Maud, musingly.

"So was this Bartlett; and I've noticed that although the Doctor can be polite enough to you young ladies, he don't put on any dancing airs with me; and he's quite particular about not sitting for his picture. However, I've sent back two very good ones to the firm, and when we return to Para I expect to hear whether he is the man. Meantime, you must excuse me if I stick rather close to your party; for it won't do for me to lose sight of the Doctor as I have of the Senhor. He is an artful dodger, he is, and he gave me the slip in Para."

"We expected to have his company up the river," said Delight. She was going to add, "and we shall probably come across him before the journey is over," but she hesitated about giving Mr. Jenkins any more clews.

"I don't see why you should care to follow the Senhor," said Maud. "He was born in Lisbon, and I assure you that his family are highly respectable. Do you know anything of this Mr. Bartlett's antecedents?"

"Oh! yes, I have his whole memoir; he was born of poor but honest parents, down in Rhode Island; he was especially bright at figures from his earliest childhood; likewise languages; he learned Portuguese when he was apprenticed to a Portuguese Jew tallow-chandler, at Padan Aram."

"So you see it could *not* have been the Senhor," Delight interrupted, confidently.

"The Senhor speaks English remarkably well," insinuated Mr. Jenkins.

"But your description is all at fault," said Delight. "Mr. Bartlett is said to have been a blond, while Senhor Silva has a remarkably dark complexion and black hair."

Mr. Jenkins replied by a significant pantomime, washing his face and hands carefully in an imaginary fluid, and remarking, sententiously, "Hair dye."

"If the Senhor is only Mr. Bartlett disguised," Maud remarked, "how could he know about my Lisbon friends, and describe them so accurately?"

"That's what gets me," replied Mr. Jenkins, "its the one extenuating circumstance in his favor, you are his best witness; it's a pity that there is n't some one to prove an alibi for the Doctor too. Do you know where he was born and bred?"

"In New Haven," said Delight promptly. "He told me so."

"He ought to have put it further off," said Mr. Jenkins.

"But he is familiar with the vicinity of Padan Aram," exclaimed Maud. "I spent a summer there, sketching, and he knew all about Nonquitt and New Bedford."

"That's where he was n't smart; nothing like a woman for the detective business."

"But then again he does not understand Portuguese very well, only a little from having been in Brazil once before."

"That's where he was a little too smart, he speaks it well."

"All this circumstantial evidence is mere nonsense," Maud announced with authority, "anyone can see that Doctor Stillman is as true and honorable as he is gentle and kind. I consider your suspicions insulting in the extreme."

"All the same, Miss Van Vechten; I shall watch him pretty close till I get him back to Para and receive my orders from headquarters."

"There is no need of resenting Mr. Jenkins' suspicions," Delight remarked quietly; "it is his business to suspect, and that he is following a false scent can do the Doctor no harm. I will guarantee that he will not attempt to elude or escape you, but that you will find his entire career perfectly open and straightforward."

"Where are the others?" Maud asked; "we have been so much absorbed in listening to Mr. Jenkins that we have not noticed where the canoeman has been taking us."

Maud, after a vigorous conversation with the Indian, elicited the information that he had been engaged by the hour, and had paddled aimlessly on, expecting to be told when to return. Mr. Jenkins consulted his watch.

"We must row at once for the steamer; the others are doubtless there, and wondering what has become of us."

"What if they have started without us," Maud exclaimed.

"Father would never allow them to do that," Delight replied. When they reached the open river they found the steamer still there, but met the Professor waiting anxiously for them on the shore.

"I did not know but I should have to land the party," he exclaimed, "and wait in Breves for the next boat. Were you lost?"

Victoria met them as they came on deck, displaying her purchases in the way of red and yellow pottery, chickens with green and blue crests and impossible tail-feathers. The Professor had some remarkable finds, too, in fossils and in antique pottery, a vulture, and a nondescript idol.

Mr. Jenkins looked about in an uneasy way. "Where is the Doctor?" he asked.

"We were so sorry!" Victoria replied: "but the woman who made the pottery was very sick, and the Doctor thought he could cure her, so he had his medicine-chest carried from the boat and stayed."

Utter silence followed Victoria's news. The steamer was making good time now up the broad river. Mr. Jenkins gave the girls an expressive look and strode away to the captain, asking if he could be put ashore. "No, indeed," replied the indignant functionary; "we wasted time enough waiting for you at Breves. We can't stop again just as we've got up steam; but I'll put you off to-morrow, if you wish it, with the greatest of pleasure."

CHAPTER V.

NEAR TO NATURE'S HEART.

ALTHOUGH Delight had defended the Doctor so warmly she was by no means so confident as she had seemed. She had a judicial mind, accustomed to weigh evidence, and not easily carried away by her feelings. That Dr. Stillman had steadily won their good opinion was not a convincing proof that he was innocent, and her kind heart was greatly troubled. She lay awake the greater part of the night, pondering the situation. Something seemed to trouble Victoria, too, for she tossed about uneasily in her hammock, which happened to be hung quite near Delight's.

"Vic," whispered the latter, after a time, "are you asleep?"

"You know I am not," Victoria replied pettishly; "you must have heard me grumbling and tumbling."

"Yes; but I did n't know but perhaps the Brazil nuts you ate for dessert might possibly have disagreed with you."

"Nonsense; my digestion is all right, but my self-respect is out of order. Come here, and sit on the side of my hammock, and I will tell you all about it."

Delight crept across in the moonlight, and Victoria began her confession.

"Do you know, Delight dear, that I believe that sick Indian was only an excuse for Dr. Stillman to leave our party?"

Delight started. "I know it," she replied: "but what makes you think so?"

"Well, you know your dear papa is quite deaf, and he was so much interested in everything about us, that the Doctor and I were as good as alone all day; and Delight, dear, I was dreadfully rude to him; and I am quite ashamed of myself, for I don't see how I

IN CONFIDENCE.

could have been so unladylike. This was how it happened. Everything was so lovely and strange in that canoe-ride that I grew quite enthusiastic, and I remember that I said it would be delightful to glide on so forever, near to Nature's heart, and away from all the artificiality of our modern society. And Dr. Stillman agreed that it would, provided that one were not quite alone, but for two people who loved each other to begin life so would be like the creation of a new heaven and a new earth. I was not sure whether he was making sport of me or whether he was really growing sentimental, and as I did not approve of either attitude, I was vexed enough; and I asked him what, in that case, would become of his fine theories of living for the benefit of the human race. Then he acknowledged that I was right; that life in such a paradise would be selfish in the extreme, and not to be wished for by any one until he had won his palm. And after that he read me another of his moral lectures about the joy of living for others, and of loving people we don't like, which I told him seemed to me an evident paradox. And he even proceeded to make a personal application of his remarks, and to beg me to choose the career for which I thought God had particularly fitted me, and in which I could do the most good in the world. Oh! I was angry. I told him that we were not all intended to be cart-horses, and hold our noses to the grindstone. By-the-by, it strikes me now that was rather a mixed metaphor, for I never saw a cart-horse do such a thing, but I don't believe he noticed it, for he did not smile, but grew quite gray about the lips, and replied that it was only his extreme interest in me which prompted him to take such a liberty. Then I informed him that it was indeed a liberty, and that he had no business to be interested in me, and that as I intended to finish my education at Vassar, I had no need of a tutor."

"O Vic, how could you have been so rude?"

"Outrageous, wasn't it?"

"Yes. I don't believe you really were as bad as that."

"Oh yes, I was; and he begged my pardon humbly enough, but he was every bit as angry as I. The spectacles came off, and his big eyes flashed, and he said I should not be troubled by any interference in future. At that moment I believe he would have liked to have rolled me in the mud, as William the Conqueror did Matilda, when she scorned him."

"I believe that, like Matilda, you would have respected him more if he had done so. What happened next?"

"Nothing in particular. We looked at the pottery, and I told the Professor that Professor Orton brought back a quantity of it, and it was in the Museum at Vassar. Then, naturally, we talked about Professor Orton and the beautiful collection of South American birds and other curiosities which he gathered with so much pains in his trip across this continent, and which Vassar now owns. I lamented that the poor man should have died just at the beginning of his career, and Dr. Stillman replied that he envied him, for he had done a definite work for science and would be remembered as a man who had accomplished something. Your father said that Vassar might be very proud of Professor Orton's memory, and then a messenger came and desired the Doctor to call on this sick person; and while we waited outside in the shade of the mangoes I cooled down a little, and realized that I had been hasty, and had possibly offended him, and determined that on our way back to the ship I would satisfy my self-respect by a not too abject apology. But when he came out he announced that he would not be able to accompany us,— this poor creature needed his attention. I was so surprised that I could not say anything. Your father hoped that he would find us at Santarem, where we intend to make our longest stop, and he promised that in case we left the town before his arrival we would leave a letter for him informing him of our next movements. 'If I am too busy to do it myself, Miss Victoria here will be my amanuensis,' your father said, and I could feel that the Doctor looked straight at me, though I would not meet his gaze. 'Very well,' he said, 'if Miss Victoria will write me of your plans, I will try to join you,' and then he went back into the house, and we came away."

"I don't see, then, what you have to worry about; you will have your opportunity to apologize, after all."

"Yes; but a written apology is so much more compromising than a spoken one. I could have made some casual remark which would not have signified much, and yet would have placed us on good terms, and now I must eat humble-pie or complicate the matter still more. Besides, if I write at all, it is the same as acknowledging that I want him to travel with us, and he was dangerously near being sentimental, and it might be encouraging him."

"Then," said Delight cheerfully, "everything seems to be for the best, just as it is."

"You are such a perverse little optimist. I really believe if you were cast into the den of lions with Daniel, you would say, ' What an uncommonly good chance to study Zoölogy!' Can't you see that everything is for the worst, — that if I do not apologize I stamp myself as wanting in every instinct of good breeding."

"Vic, dear," — Delight spoke a little lower, and drew her arm closer about her friend. "I was thinking of something else when I said that everything was probably for the best. While you were talking with the Doctor, Mr. Jenkins made a rather startling communication to us girls. He thinks that the Doctor is that defaulting cashier in disguise."

Victoria grasped her friend's hand tightly. — "The idiot!"

"Why, Vic, you were the first to suggest the idea."

"Yes; but that was before I really became acquainted with Dr. Stillman. Does he impress you as a scoundrel?"

"No, dear. I can hardly imagine that any one could be enough of a hypocrite to wear such a face as Dr. Stillman's over a black heart; but I should hesitate to trust my own impressions in a case like this."

"You are too self-distrustful and cautious. People who weigh both sides so evenly end by never having any opinion of their own. Now I *always* trust to my intuitions."

"And you are sometimes mistaken."

"Better to be honestly mistaken than to be forever on the fence, hesitating, doubting, balancing."

"Well, Vic, even supposing Dr. Stillman to be perfectly innocent, it seems to me that it is fortunate that he is not subjected to the espionage and dogging of this detective."

"I do not agree with you. It seems to me that his leaving us at this juncture will be regarded by this narrow-minded creature as a suspicious circumstance, while, if he had stayed, even Mr. Jenkins would have seen that he was entirely on the wrong track."

"Vie, dear, don't worry about it; everything will come straight, I am sure."

"And this letter, which I am to write the Doctor at Santarem?"

"Never cross a bridge till you come to it. You will know just what to do when the time comes."

Life on the steamer passed tranquilly and pleasantly. The girls began to understand why it was proper to speak of this intricate network of braided watercourses as the Amazons, and not as one river. The steamer, to avoid the swift

MR. JENKINS' OPPONENT AT CARDS

current, hugged the shore, giving them a fine view of the rank vegetation, the lowlands covered with thousands of cattle, and the woods matted together with looping lianas and parasitic plants.

Mr. Jenkins left the steamer at its next stopping-place, Monte Alegre, or the Joyous Mountain. At their last view of him he was playing cards with a priest, but his sneak-box was on his knees, and one wary eye kept watch on the steamboat landing. He announced his intention of remaining here until the arrival of the next boat bound down the river, when he would return to Breves. Near Monte Alegre they visited a cacao orchard, and saw the process of drying the fruit from which chocolate is made. It grows in oblong shells eight or ten inches in length. The outer casing is broken with hammers, and the clusters of seeds inside — each seed the size of an Italian chestnut — are separated and dried in the sun. The girls were helped to delicious chocolate, made from the roasted and powdered kernels. The beverage was beaten with a twirling stick until light and frothy, and Maud declared that even at Maillard's she had never tasted a more appetizing preparation of chocolate.

Here, too, they witnessed the manufacture of farinha, which serves the natives in the place of bread. They had been served with it on the steamer, a dish of it being placed before each passenger. The girls had provoked the merriment of the natives by helping themselves to the mass, which resembled toasted crumbs, by means of a spoon. The Brazilians, with a dexterity of touch truly surprising, would take a pinch of the crumbs in their fingers and throw it into their mouths with great accuracy of aim, while the hand was at quite a distance. They now saw the farinha made from the manioc root, which is first soaked in pools of water, then scraped and grated, passed through a sieve, after having had the poisonous juice expressed from it, and roasted on large ovens of stone or copper. Tapioca is a preparation of the juice.

They climbed together the Serra of Erere, a mountain at the back of the town of Monte Alegre, from which a wide-spreading view was obtained of the surrounding country, and visited the Indian village of the same name, noted for its hammock-weaving, where they lingered for several days. These hammocks are made by the Indian women, not of grasses, like the ones sent to us, but of cotton, the main part closely woven in the shape of a square, six feet across. Sometimes, by the use of a dyed thread, a simple, decorative pattern was introduced. The cotton the women used was of their own raising and

OLD CRONE SPINNING.

preparation. The girls were struck by the odd sounds issuing from the houses, as of children beating upon drums, but ascertained, on visiting the dwellings, that these sounds were caused by the light palm wands deftly handled by the Indian girls as they beat the cotton to fleecy lightness.

Maud made a sketch of an old crone spinning at a clumsy, aboriginal wheel. She was busy everywhere during their brief stay, and all were interested in this primitive, wild life. The Indians were gentle and hospitable, not at all reminding them of the female warriors from whom the mighty river was named.

Delight whispered slyly to Victoria, as they marked the simplicity and poverty of the household furnishing. "This is certainly living 'near to Nature's heart,' but does it strike you, dear, that you would greatly enjoy it?"

No, Victoria hardly thought she would; but Maud, with an artist's instinct, seemed to get at the spirit of it all. She made friends with the little naked Indian children, whom she painted as they disported themselves at their morning bath by the side of the beautiful palm-shaded spring. Her knowledge of Portuguese made it possible for her to converse with those of the older women who understood the language. She was a close observer, and none of the others noticed, as she did, that the Indian children loved the water, while the negro babies cried when they were bathed; the little darkies slept in the full glare of the sunlight, and the Indians carefully selected the shade.

The Indians were religious as well as kindly. They had taken easily to the religion of the Jesuits, but some of their barbaric superstitions still remained. One night there occurred an eclipse of the moon. No daily journal had warned the public of the event, and the girls were too far from the Vassar observatory to receive special notification from Miss Mitchell. The shadow had advanced some way upon the moon before their attention was drawn to it. The villagers, more prompt in making the discovery, began to thump with their pestles in the large farinha mortars, and to send off rockets, and fire guns.

"What is the meaning of all this racket?" Maud inquired. "Have

INDIAN IDEA OF AN ECLIPSE.

we chanced upon the Brazilian Fourth of July, or is this the fête of some more than usually illustrious saint?"

The Professor explained that the Indians were exorcising an evil spirit who had stolen the moon's food. "The Indians believe," said he, "that every few weeks a young moon is born; its growth is constant and rapid, and finally it reaches its full, obese middle age; then, like man, it grows no longer, but becomes daily thinner until it fades away and dies, and its place is supplied by its offspring. Now when an eclipse occurs they attribute the diminished form to the deprivation of the daily allowance of farinha, which some tricky spirit has stolen away. Then, to encourage the dying moon, and to compel the evil spirit to restore the food, two operations are necessary: first, the beating of farinha in the great family mortar, and second, the shooting of rockets and firearms to scare the fiend who is causing the mischief. This belief is confirmed by the moon's recovery following their exertions.

"That is all very interesting to me," Maud remarked. "I remember hearing that our North American Indians believe that during an eclipse a dog is eating the moon, and they fall to beating every unlucky cur that can be found in their camp as long as it continues. I wish I might learn more of their superstitions, and I am sorry that our stay in Erere is to be so short."

"We are likely to live among other tribes some time," replied the Professor, "and you will have plenty of opportunity to indulge your fancy."

A few days later found them once more ploughing the yellow waters of the Amazons, bound for Santarem, on the southern shore, where an unlooked-for meeting awaited them.

As they steamed rapidly along the intricate maze of watercourses, confiding in the sagacity of the native pilot to decide on the proper channel, Victoria happened to say that she did not wonder that so many of the early explorers lost their way, and failed in their attempts to ascend the Amazons.

This started the Professor off in a panegyric of these same voyagers.

"Ah!" he exclaimed, "it is difficult for us now to realize their sufferings as they wandered up and down, struggling against wind and current for weary weeks and months, searching for El Dorado.

Few romances rival their thrilling experiences. Have you ever heard the story of Madame Odonais?"

"Never," Maud replied, conscious that she lowered herself in the Professor's esteem by this confession of her ignorance, but anxious to be enlightened.

"In 1769 Madame Godin des Odonais descended the Amazons in order to join her husband, who was in Cayenne, and had sent her word of a Portuguese boat which would meet her at Tabatinga and convey her to him. She set out from Quito with her two brothers, a French physician, her nephew — a lad of ten years of age, a negro slave, and three women servants. They came over the Andes to the Bobonnassa River; here the muleteers who had brought them over the mountains left them and returned. The doctor and the negro slave went on to an Indian village for boatmen and canoes, while the others camped beside the river awaiting their return. They never came, having probably lost their way and perished in the wilderness. The others, after waiting for twenty-five days, concluded to build a raft and venture down the river. This raft shortly after went to pieces, all their provisions were lost, and they themselves narrowly escaped drowning. In this desperate condition they attempted to follow down the banks of the river on foot, but in three or four days all died of starvation with the exception of Madame Odonais, who wandered on, subsisting on fruit and some partridge eggs which she found. So she strayed for eight days, when she came across two Indians launching a canoe, who kindly took her down the river to Andoas, from which place she obtained conveyance to Tabatinga, where she found the Portuguese vessel waiting, and was carried to her husband."

"What a terrible experience!" Victoria mused; "I should have gone insane."

"She was delirious much of the time, and her husband writes, 'The remembrance of the terrible spectacles, the horror of solitude, and the darkness of night in the desert, had such an effect on her mind that her hair turned gray.'"

"But all this terrible privation was experienced before she really reached the Amazons," Maud said. "Pray, tell us about the early explorers, who sailed with astonishment up its broad flood — four miles across from bank to bank. Joaquin Miller describes it rightly when he says:

>"'It was dark and dreadful! Wide like an ocean,
>Much like a river, but more like a sea.'

"It is really the Mediterranean of South America."

"It is one of my theories," said the Professor, "a theory which I hope to prove on this expedition, that the lower valley of the Amazons, bed and entire flood-plain, was once an arm of the ocean which the river sediment has gradually built up above the level of the sea, though so slightly that the tides are felt as far up as Obidos. I shall look carefully for marine fossils to confirm this opinion."

"This was not Agassiz's theory," Maud remarked, in a deprecatory way.

"True," the Professor replied; "and one must be very sure in his convictions to oppose the great geologist. Professor Agassiz supposed that the Amazonian valley is a gigantic furrow ploughed through the continent by a glacier descending eastward from the Andes, and spreading a vast moraine; that the entire region was above water during the tertiary period. But Professor Orton found tertiary shells at Tabatinga."

"The glacier idea is a magnificent one," said Victoria, enthusiastically, "but whether the valley is a trench scooped by such a Titanic agency, or a true Mediterranean, which has gradually lifted itself, changing from a marine to an earth life, it gives us an inspiring notion of the growth and movement in the nature which we are accustomed to call inanimate."

"You will find the history of the exploration of the river equally interesting," said the Professor. "The discoverers called it a freshwater sea, Santa Maria de la Mar Dulce. This name was changed to the Amazons by Orellana, one of Pizarro's soldiers, who descended the river from Peru in 1540 and 1541, and told marvellous tales of the female warriors to be found upon its banks. To the Jesuits, however, is due the greatest honor, for they were true missionaries in those early days, and civilization followed where they planted the cross. Pedro Cristoval de Acuna gives the first record of their work. They perfected the *lingua geral*, and to them is due its prevalence instead of a multitude of Indian dialects along the entire length of the river. They explored, and baptized, and taught, and practised the healing art, many of our valuable medicines having been discovered by them. Quinine was first known as Jesuit powder. They fought against the barbarous instincts of the savages on one side; against cannibalism and vice in the Indians; and against the rapacity and cruelty of the conquerors; against the murder, and robbery, and slavery practised by the Spaniards and Portuguese. They were heroes; and, Protestant that I am, I do not know that I rejoice in their expulsion from the land, especially as no better system of religion than theirs has taken its place."

"You are really eloquent, father," Delight said. "Do you wish you were one of those old Jesuits?"

"No, my dear," he replied gravely. "Science has its martyrs today, and it is honor enough to be one of them. How many men of education and genius, with their hearts on fire with a love of nature, have perished nobly here!— Orton, in the lonely Andes, Hartt, at Rio, with others of European origin; and many besides, who brought back with them the seeds of death, and deemed the penalty a slight one for the privilege of having contributed to the world's advancement. May my life be as useful, and my last end like theirs."

There was a little hush about him. The time was coming when

INDIANS SINGING MASS.

these words would be remembered with added significance, and again
Maud noticed how very frail he seemed. Was there strength enough
there to carry him through any unforeseen privations or excitement
which might await them on this trip? All of a sudden the journey
struck her as a hazardous experiment. He might have lived ten or
fifteen years longer in happy tranquillity; why had he taken such risks
in the evening of his life? Then she realized that the stories he had
been telling them were of past centuries; there could be no danger in
such commonplace voyaging as this,— and while she mused there
was a cry of interest by those looking forward, and Victoria exclaimed that they were in sight of Santarem.

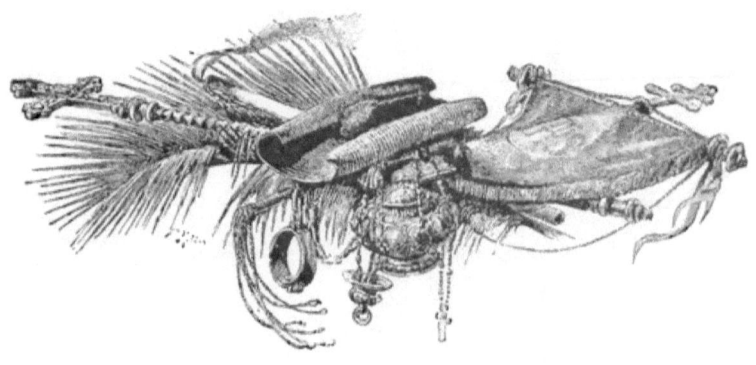

CHAPTER VI.

THE FAZENDA DA SILVA.

THEY were at Santarem, the most important city in the interior of Brazil, and to reach it the steamer had made a turn out of the turbid water of the Amazons, two miles up the black Tapajos. As it lay in the deep water, waiting for boatmen to take the Professor and his party ashore, the girls had a fine panorama of the *cidade* glistening white in the noonday sun, and the palm-thatched roofs of the humbler cottages clustered along the shore. Negresses were laundering their linen in the river, their gay turbans and neckerchiefs making bright spots of color in the centre of the dazzling white of the heaped-up washing. There was little passing in the streets, for the steamer had arrived at the beginning of the afternoon siesta, when business stagnates and all social life ceases. Even the Indian canoemen were coiled up in the shade, and had it not been for the sun-loving African element the place might have passed for the court of the Sleeping Beauty. A lusty whistle from the steamer woke a slight pretence of activity among the wharf loungers, and a canoe put out to the vessel.

"There is no hotel in the place," the Professor remarked, "nor anywhere in the interior, and we must inquire of the principal store-keeper where to ask the hospitality of a couple of rooms in which to hang our hammocks."

The boatman directed them to the shop of Senhor Correa, and here they were met by the Senhor's valet, a barefooted but polite mulatto, who, on hearing the Professor's name, assured them that they were expected, and that rooms had been provided for them, but hoped they would excuse his master, as he was now taking his siesta, until dinner at four, when he would be most happy to meet them.

"What does it mean?" Mrs. Holmes asked. "I never heard of such princely hospitality. Does he welcome every stranger in this cordial fashion?"

"It is evidently a mistake," the Professor replied. "He is expecting some other guests, and the servant fancies that we are the ones."

But there stood the valet bowing, smiling, beckoning them to follow, and declaring that his master's house was at "suas ordens" and at the end of the store there was a tempting vista of a courtyard shaded by

"The banana with leaf like a tent."

"It is a fortunate mistake for us; let us profit by it," counselled Victoria. "We can pay the Senhor for his hospitality when all is explained," and handing her bags to the servant she followed him into the court, which she found encircled by verandahs which led to shady sleeping-apartments. The others acted upon Victoria's example, greatly wondering and amused. The mulatto added to their bewilderment by informing them that "their friend" had sent his pleasure-boat, manned by negroes and commanded by his steward, every day at six precisely for a week past, to inquire whether they had arrived, and to convey them up the Tapajos to his fazenda.

"Who can this guardian spirit be, who is so interested in our welfare?" Maud asked, quite wild with curiosity. But the valet could not remember his name, and there seemed to be nothing to do but to hang their hammocks and to wait future developments. These came when, refreshed by a bath, they were ushered into a pretty dining room and met their courteous host. He explained that Senhor José Ignacio da Palacios had purchased a fazenda several miles up the Tapajos, and that he had charged Senhor Correa to entertain them until he could bring them within the scope of his own hospitality.

Still the mystery remained, Who was this Senhor Palacios who had anticipated their wants so thoughtfully? After the lingering dinner the Professor looked over the mail which he had ordered sent here, and there was a disappointed look on Delight's face as she glanced over her father's shoulder at the various letters.

"I thought," she said in a low voice to Victoria, "that there might be one from the Doctor. He knew we were coming here and he has had time to send a letter."

"He is right in thinking that it is my place to indicate if I care to continue the acquaintance," Victoria replied.

"I don't see what that has to do with his friendship with Papa," Delight rejoined, "he need not drop us all on your account. Mr. Jenkins would say it has a bad look, as if he wished to cover his tracks, you know."

At this point their host proposed that they should visit the church, as half an hour would probably elapse before the arrival of Senhor Palacios' boat. They walked across the square, pausing to notice an Indian child asleep under the shadow of the cross, which is always one of the features in every South American plaza. The church was rather a pretentious structure, its only claim to interest being the gilded Christ on the cross, which was sent from Munich by the naturalist Martius, who, as the quaint inscription relates, "was saved by Divine Pity from the fury of the Amazonian waves, near the Village of Santarem, and as a Monument of his Pious Gratitude to the All Powerful, ordered this Crucifix to be erected in this Church of Nossa Senhora du Conceicao, in the year 1846."

On leaving the church they walked toward the beach. A long canoe with a *tolda*, or covered space in the after part, propelled by Indian paddlers, rounded the point and drifted to the shore. A mulatto stepped from it and approached them, letter in hand. Senhor Correa explained that

CHILD ASLEEP IN THE SHADOW OF THE CROSS.

this was the steward of Senhor Palacios, and the Professor, taking the letter and finding that it was really addressed to him, opened and read it. It was signed José Ignacio da Palacios y Silva. The mystery was solved; their unknown good genius was really Senhor Silva. "The Portuguese and Brazilians rejoice in an abundance of names," the Professor explained.

"Yes," Maud replied, "I have seen as many as eight fastened to one insignificant person. The Senhor's brother whom I knew in

Lisbon, had a double family name also, but it was Sonza y Silva. I don't see why it should be different."

The Senhor made it plain for them when they met. Silva was their father's name, and he had twice married, Palacios was the maiden name of the Senhor's mother, and Sonza that of his stepmother; it was the fashion to retain the mother's name with the father's and even to drop the father's when the mother's was more noble.

SENHOR PALACIOS' VALET.

He had used both, until, on coming to Santarem he had found that Silva was so common a name in this vicinity that it would undoubtedly give rise to confusion, and so he had adopted for convenience' sake the more distinctive and distinguished name of Palacios, which it was really his right to bear. It was all plain enough after the Senhor had made it clear, but as they voyaged up the river, Victoria persisted that if the Doctor had taken an alias in this way Delight would have thought it very suspicious.

Delight had not told Victoria that Mr. Jenkins had indeed suspected the Senhor; she would have given as a reason that it did it not seem worth while, since Maud's acquaintance with his relatives vouched for his identity. She was silent now, apparently absorbed in a contemplation of the landscape. They had turned to the south, and the broad expanse of the Tapajos spread out like a lake before them. Forests were interspersed with sandy beaches, and on the further bank were rocky bluffs. The men had put up a sail and were resting on their oars as the boat raced along before a stiff breeze from the north. They passed several cattle fazendas and stopped before a picturesque group of houses, in a little grove of Javary palms. In the group on the beach they all recognized Senhor Silva in his broad

Panama hat and suit of spotless white linen. He shook hands warmly with the Professor, gave one arm to Mrs. Holmes and one to Victoria, and did his best to answer all the questions that were rained upon him. The fazenda was a new purchase. He had heard of it at Para and had immediately become its half owner with the Baron of Boavista. Taking into account the fact that he had only been on the spot two weeks he had really accomplished wonders. There had been a saw-mill here, but work had been discontinued either from want of capital or lack of enterprise; but enough of both were now to be supplied, and he took them into the long, low building and showed them the new steam machinery which had been substituted for the clumsy water power. He had purchased, he said, a little cargo steamer which he had sent up the river to Diamantina, and Itaiuba for logs. He intended to interest the Indians in the collection of the choice varieties, and to form wood yards at various points. He was full of enthusiasm at the prospect before him, and the darkness came down as they stood chatting beside the great saws. Then he led them to the cottage which he had prepared for their reception, a one-story adobe building roofed with red tiles, but so overgrown with flowering creepers, crimson, purple, white, and passion vines, which he had transplanted from the woods, that it seemed a bower of beauty. A broad hall running through the building and open at each end divided the apartment of the Professor and his wife from that of the girls. The interior was fresh and new, floored and ceiled with the first planking turned out by the saw-mill, in alternate strips of white and red cedar. There was a bedstead in Mrs. Holmes' room, for she could never accustom herself to the use of the hammock, and a queer writing-desk for the Professor. On the girls' side there were rattan sofas and easy chairs, a case of stuffed birds, hammocks, and a profusion of flowers. There was an Indian squatting on a mat outside the door, whom the Senhor introduced to Professor Holmes as Pedro the Professor's body servant, and a smiling nut-brown girl in a dark dress and white apron adorned with the effective Indian lace, was Philomena, the young ladies' maid. "I hope you will be very happy here," he said in an impersonal way, as though addressing the entire party, but Delight saw that he shot a stealthy glance at Victoria and she believed that all these preparations were for her sake.

They were awakened next morning by Philomena noiselessly removing the shutters from the unglazed windows. "Where are we?" Victoria asked sleepily.

"In fairy land!" Maud replied, "only look through that window at that mass of blossoms, bromelias, orchids, ferns, cecropias, fuchsias, cape jessamines, and sensitive plants. It is a little paradise."

The girls hastened to dress and explore their surroundings, as they had not been able to do in the dusk of the late evening. All this luxuriance of bloom seemed to be massed about their cottage, while the larger house, the Senhor's residence, stood near the saw-mill with only a shuttlecock-shaped ubassu palm to shade it.

"It is very plain," said Delight, "that he has had all these beautiful things transplanted from the forest especially to adorn our cottage. What extravagance it is."

"But they do not cost anything here," Victoria replied.

"They cost time and labor," Delight observed.

"And good taste," Maud added. "He has arranged everything with the skill of a landscape gardener."

Philomena now informed them that the Senhor would be happy to see them at breakfast, which was spread in the open air under the ubassu palm, one of whose pendant branches swayed by a little negro served as a punkah and kept away all disturbing insects.

Mrs. Holmes complimented the Senhor on his cook, for first they were served to excellent turtle soup, then to tapir steak, which the Professor pronounced as juicy and tender as beef.

"The animal was shot by my own hunters," explained the Senhor, "if you would enjoy a hunt you shall have one while you are here;"

ORCHIDS, ETC.

and he pressed them to try the potted birds which formed the next dish. Then came an arrowroot custard, flavored with vanilla from orchids growing on his own place, fried bananas, gapotis and other fruits and excellent coffee.

As the breakfast progressed he unfolded plans for their amusement, which if fully carried out would have detained them for a month.

"We must have a night's fishing by torchlight, it is great sport,

HEAD OF SWIMMING TAPIR.

and a trip to one of the interior lakes to see the Victoria Regia. I have heard of a spot where it grows in great profusion. Then we must make an excursion for birds; you have a few specimens in your cottage of the varieties to be found in this region. When my steamer returns I want to take you up to Diamantina. I believe there are some fossils up that way which may interest the Professor. And we certainly must have a jaguar hunt. The tiger-shooting you read about in 'Mr. Isaacs' is nothing to it. We must secure several fine skins for you to carry back to the States as trophies."

"My dear fellow," the Professor began, in mild expostulation; but the Senhor would not hear him. He had begun to chat with Maud about the native woods. "I believe you mentioned that you had studied wood-carving at the school in Cincinnati. You are the most wonderful person; it seems to me you have been everywhere and studied everything. I have a collection of over a hundred different kinds of woods in my office, and I would like to have your opinion as to which are the best adapted for carving, and which for marquetry."

Then he turned to the Professor again, and recollected to have heard that a settler from the Southern States, a near neighbor of his, had a fine collection of insects which it might be worth his trouble to see. Pedro would show him over that very morning; he could rest there during the heat of the day, and be back in time for the fishing which he had planned for that night. The Professor acceded readily to this plan, and after seeing him off the others were ushered into the office, where Maud found not only the specimens but a neat little turning-lathe, and several chisels and gouges ready to her hand. She examined their keen edges with the appreciation of an expert, while the Senhor talked entertainingly of wonderful examples of wood-carving which he had seen in Europe, and told effectively a little fairy story of an oak that longed to bear tulips, and how at last, when the tree was felled, a skilful carver cut the flowers from its heart.

Maud looked up from the beautiful bit of *mara coatiara*, or striped wood, which she was testing, and thought that the Senhor was really a very entertaining man.

"What a pity," he said, "that Walter Scott could not have had you, Miss Maud, to realize his pretty fancy for a set of chessmen."

"What was that?" Victoria asked.

THE COTTAGE AT THE FAZENDA.

"Don't you remember? He writes in his autobiography," — and the Senhor drew from his pocket a note-book, and read: "'Wherever I went I cut a piece of a branch from a tree; these constituted what I called my log-book; and I intended to have a set of chessmen out of them, each having reference to the place where it was cut — as the kings from Falkland and Holy Rood; the queens from Queen Mary's yew tree, at Crookston; the bishops from abbeys or Episcopal palaces; the knights from baronial residences; the rooks from royal fortresses; and the pawns generally from places worthy of historical note.'"

Maud was struck with the idea. "I have a friend, Barbara Featherstonhaugh, in England," she said, "who will get me the woods, and I will do it. I wish I had known of it when I was abroad, there were so many interesting places which we visited in Spain and Portugal. Think of a bishop from the Escurial, a knight from one of Bobadil's yew trees at Granada, a black king from the old Moorish castle at Cintra. Oh! that would be the very thing! I could carve all the black pieces to represent Moors, and the white should be Ferdinand and Isabella and their followers. Senhor Silva, will you not write to your sister to send me some bits of wood from that old Moorish ruin at Cintra?"

The Senhor for some reason seemed for a moment quite embarrassed by this simple request. He hesitated, changed color, but quickly recovered himself and agreed to do so.

"If it is any trouble I will do it myself," Maud said. "I would quite enjoy writing your sister and telling her how we happened to meet you."

"I beg you will allow me to do it," the Senhor replied hastily. "I have intended writing home for a week past, but have been so busy putting everything in order. I want to persuade my family to emigrate since I have purchased this place. I think I can make them very comfortable here. There is really very good society at Santarem, and some of the wealthier fazenda proprietors are gentlemen. I have an invitation for you all to a dinner, from their illustriousnesses the Baron and Baroness of Boavista. Don't you think that ladies of cultivation might be happy even in this wild place?"

Again his remark was an impersonal one; but he looked at Victoria as he spoke, and Victoria, feeling herself addressed, answered, — "Certainly; the place is a perfect paradise. I should think one might be happy here forever, provided one's friends were with one."

Somehow the remark sounded very much like the one from the Doctor which had so offended her, and, realizing this, Victoria blushed, though angry with herself for doing so.

Leaving Maud with her carving the Senhor led the others into the garden. There were ferns here which he thought might interest Delight, and they would make a botanizing expedition to the woods in a few days for more.

"You seem to have provided for the amusement of every one," Victoria said. "One would fancy that you were determined on making us all in love with the place."

"I wish I could discover what would interest you in it," he replied.

"Have you not heard? I have developed a scientific mania for palms."

"Good. There are several species peculiar to the Tapajos. I do not think you will find the Jara elsewhere. Has Philomena shown you her lace work? It is really curious. I thought you might care to take lessons from her. This Indian lace will be a novelty to introduce to your decorative art friends at home. You see that I feel that I must make you happy here as long as I can, for I shall be desperately lonely after you have gone."

The Professor returned at night enthusiastic but quite tired out. The collection of insects which he had seen was really a remarkable one, embracing many new species. He must go there again, and take Maud with him to make drawings. He had had one entomological experience on his way home which was not very pleasant, having crossed the line of march of a company of fire ants, which had stung his ankles unmercifully.

"They are one of the pests of this region," the Senhor explained; "and by the way, have you never heard that they act an important part in the native wedding ceremony?"

No one knew of this, and he told them entertainingly that when an Indian wished to marry he was submitted to the ordeal of having his hand tied up in a bag of fire ants, his endurance of the pain proving his fitness for the trials of matrimony.

The Professor laughed,—"I certainly have suffered more this afternoon," he said, "than in all the twenty years of my married life."

His feet were so swollen that it was necessary to put him to bed, and to defer the fishing excursion until another evening; and this the Senhor seemed very willing to do, though he was profuse in his polite regrets for the Professor's misfortune.

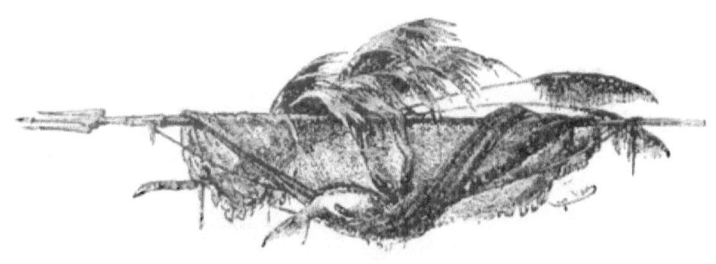

CHAPTER VII.

QUEER FISH.

THE days drifted by so pleasantly at the Fazenda da Silva that a fortnight passed before anyone had realized it. The fishing excursion took place in the second week.

The night was calm and splendid, the sky full of stars, and the air of glancing fireflies. Both were repeated in the black water of the river, and the reflections were so intermingled that it seemed to the observer that the stars danced about him. They were in two canoes, — Graciliano, the best fisherman on the place, the Senhor, Delight, and Victoria in the first, and Pedro, the Professor, Mrs. Holmes, and Maud in the second. Each boat was manned with Indian paddlers. Graciliano and Pedro stood in the bow, each with a waving torch in his left hand and a long trident in his right. The Senhor's fisherman is falsely named the graceful, Maud thinks, for a more misshapen monster she has rarely seen. He has a squat figure, his neck is awry, he is squint-eyed and pock-marked, and a part of one foot has been bitten off by a poisonous water-snake. But he can spear fish if he is no beauty, and his brawny arm shakes his palm torch until the sparks mingle with the dancing stars and fly to meet their reflections in the water. And as the sparks hiss and die into blackness with that fiery kiss, a fish leaps, the trident descends unerringly, and a huge fish flounders in the bottom of the boat near Victoria's feet. She gives a quick, nervous movement, and might have fallen into the water, but the Senhor steadies her; and she seats herself further back in the boat. The Senhor stands erect. He is drawing a great iron-wood bow, and is looking over the water for something at which to aim. A dark object rises silently at some distance; the arrow whizzes across the water; there is an angry snort, and an alligator sinks wounded below the water. The paddlers guide the boat out of the broad sheet of moonlight close to the bank, where the assai palms throw a dense shadow on the water, and here Graciliano shakes his firebrand until he looks a very Pluto — god of darkness and fire — and the fishes leap to their death and struggle in the bottom of the boat.

GRACILIANO SPEARING FISH.

They are queer objects, certainly, and the Professor regards them with much interest. "Nowhere in the world," he remarks to Maud, "are there stranger or more varied forms. Agassiz reported the startling fact that the variety of fish in the Amazons is twice as great as in the Mediterranean, and a larger number than the Atlantic from one pole to another."

"How many species are there?" Maud asked, half indifferently, for she is more interested in the brilliant scene than in icthyology.

"Eighteen hundred to two thousand. It is well that the waters are so prolific, for the natives live almost entirely upon fish. The *pirarucu* more than takes the place with them of our codfish. It is a huge fish from ten to thirteen feet long, with a plate armor of great scales bordered with a red line, and its odor when salted is not of roses."

Mrs. Holmes did not speak much; she was silently battling with her old enemies the mosquitoes. "Was it not Professor Orton?" Maud asked, "who was reminded here of Midshipman Wilberforce's

THE PIRARUCU.

apostrophe, — 'Ye greedy animals I am ashamed of you. Cannot you once forego your dinner and feast your mind with the poetry of the landscape.'"

Suddenly the boats were surrounded by a school of leaping creatures larger than any of the fish yet speared. Graciliano threw his trident into the bottom of the boat and sat down.

"What are they?" Victoria asked in some alarm, "not sharks?"

"No, indeed, sharks never come up here," replied the Senhor. "they are only dolphins; but the Indians have a superstition that dolphins can change themselves into men, and that they often do so and commit a great deal of mischief. The only way which you can detect them is to look at their feet, which have the trifling peculiarity of being turned backward. Graciliano would not dare to incur the anger of these backward-walking pixies, for fear that they might carry off his wife, or take revenge upon him in some other way."

"How very curious," Victoria said; "will he not tell us more about them? Please ask him, Senhor Silva, and see what he will say."

But Graciliano, on being questioned, only hung his head sheepishly and said they were queer fish; she must ask the Indian women about them.

"Philomena will be more communicative," said the Senhor. "There are many myths about the dolphins: some say that they are in love with the Indian girls, and it is for their sake that they assume human shape; and there is another more obscure tradition which makes them sons of the Amazons, which those cruel dames drowned in the river, wishing only to rear their daughters and perpetuate a race of female warriors."

"Poor enchanted princes," mused Victoria. "I did not know the Indians had such poetical fancies."

"How strange it is," Delight remarked, "that that myth about the Amazons should be so widely spread. Columbus believed it, and so did Sir Walter Raleigh, and yet it is manifestly an importation of an old-world fable."

"With the shadows looming about so mysteriously, and the torch-lights flaring and flickering so weirdly, I am inclined to believe in the myth," said Victoria. "See, the dolphins have vanished; it is because they have caught a glimpse of their warrior mothers in their cuirasses of plated gold, and — O Senhor Silva, what *is* that creature?" for Graciliano had speared a very ugly customer indeed, — a dogfish, with savage teeth.

They moored their boats shortly after on a sandy beach, and built a bonfire under a clump of palms. Here they ate the supper which they had brought with them, and told stories and chatted, while the shells of the Brazil nuts which they threw into the fire snapped and crackled. Then they drifted home in the early morning, the girls singing Lord Lytton's Boat Song of Lake Como. Softly the sweet voices echoed and died on the broad lake-like expanse of the Tapajos, and the stars and fireflies danced with their reflections in time to the rhythm.

> "The beautiful lake, the Larian lake!
>   Soft lake like a silver sea,
> The Huntress Queen, with her nymphs of sheen,
>   Never had bath like thee;
> See, the Lady of Night and her maids of light
>   Even now are mid-deep in thee."

"Good night," said the Senhor, "*noche clara y serena.*"

The next morning Maud spent in making drawings of the fish for the Professor. Pedro trudged several times from the boat to the house with as much as he could carry. The Senhor found her at her work.

"You do not look as if you enjoyed this," he ventured.

"No," she replied; "it is not very artistic work. If Mr. Jenkins were only here with his camera!"

"The saints forbid!" the Senhor exclaimed hastily.

"You do not like Mr. Jenkins?" Maud asked.

"He is a queer fish," the Senhor replied evasively.

And that afternoon he made the same remark of another of their fellow-voyagers. He came upon Delight and Victoria, who, with Philomena, were attempting to penetrate a little way into the forest. Delight was looking for ferns as usual, but Victoria was following up a salsaparilla vine.

PEDRO RETURNING FROM FISHING.

"I am trying to learn all I can about the medicinal plants," she said, "Dr. Stillman interested me in them."

"Yes," the Senhor replied indifferently; and then he remarked, as he had of Mr. Jenkins, "The Doctor was a queer fish."

"He is a very agreeable gentleman," Victoria replied hotly. "I was desperately ignorant about Brazilian botany, and he made it very fascinating to me. Do you know the *guarana* shrub? He told me I would find it on the Tapajos. The Indians make a drug from the seeds, which takes the place with them of quinine."

The Senhor had never heard of *guarana*, but Philomena knew it well, and promised to obtain some cakes of it for her. From her description it resembled chocolate, and was often moulded into the shape of turtles or fishes.

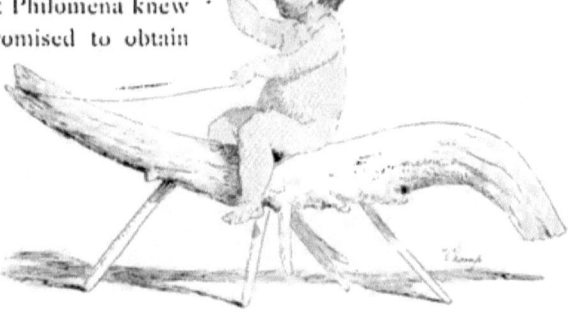

INDIAN CHILD'S HOBBY-HORSE.

"It seems to me very odd," Victoria said, "that you, a native of the country, should know less about its products than the Doctor, who is a stranger here."

The Senhor flushed angrily, and Victoria felt that she had been rude once more, and hastened to explain that she presumed it was because this was a matter only interesting to physicians.

Delight regarded the Senhor keenly with her calm, judicial eyes. It was evident that he did not like the Doctor, and this added weight to her own distrust.

She determined to have a talk with Maud, and so, after dinner, while Philomena was bleaching linen by the river (for the Senhor did not believe in the Portuguese proverb, " As dirty as a tablecloth "), and Victoria was reading aloud to the Professor from the Annals of the Hakluyt Society, Delight was glad to see Maud lay aside the sketch she had been making of a little Indian boy playing at hobby-horse with an irregular tree-root near the sawmill, and announce her intention of writing a letter. Delight followed her to the cottage, remarking carelessly, as Maud arranged her writing-materials, " The Senhor seems to have formed a prejudice against the Doctor."

" Um," said Maud.

" What did you remark, dear?" inquired Delight.

" Nothing. I was only thinking that he seems to be prejudiced against Mr. Jenkins as well."

" Well, what does that go to prove?"

" Nothing. I wish it did."

" Maud, don't you think the Senhor is very partial to Victoria?"

" Yes; and so was the Doctor."

" That may explain his prejudice."

" Very satisfactorily, to my mind, but it does not account for his antipathy to Mr. Jenkins."

" None of us are very fond of Mr. Jenkins. I wonder whether Victoria likes the Senhor."

" I hope not."

" Why? Don't you think it would be very nice? Think what a magnificent place this could be made; and of course they would live in New York part of the time; and Mr. Delavan could come down here just as well as not. I think it would be charming."

" I do not. I had much rather she would fancy the Doctor."

" With all Mr. Jenkins's suspicions."

" A fig for Mr. Jenkins. I like the Doctor, while this plausible, popular Senhor is altogether too fine for me."

"Maud Van Vechten! when you know all of his family."

"Very good families sometimes have very disreputable sons. I am certain that the Silvas would have referred to this brother in America if there had not been some good reason, and I am writing to Candida at this present moment. I believe that she will tell me the truth, and I reserve my opinion of the Senhor until her answer arrives."

Maud wrote a long time, and when her letter was finished she placed it in Philomena's possession, requesting her to send it with the other letters from the Fazenda to the post-office at Santarem. Philomena placed the letter upon the desk in her master's office, and if Maud could have looked into the room late that night she would have seen a curious and not a reassuring sight. The Senhor entered the room after bidding his guests good-night, lit a cigar, and proceeded to write a letter. He caught sight, as he wrote, of Maud's letter lying beside him, and tossed it carelessly into the mail-bag. Then he wrote more slowly, evidently not thinking of the words which his fingers traced. Finally he laid down his pen, took out the letter, and studied the address. Then he moistened the envelope and waited until it softened sufficiently to allow of his carefully opening it. He next read the letter from beginning to end. A scornful smile curled his mustachios as he finished and placed it in a little brass dish destined to receive cigar ashes. He lit the letter, and as it flashed into flame the smile on his face was still more unpleasant to look upon.

CHAPTER VIII.

ON THE TRAIL.

MR. JENKINS sat behind the church at Monte Alegre and played cards steadily with the *curé*, but his thoughts took a wider range than the cards which he held in his hand. He glanced expectantly up the river for the faint thread of smoke which would tell him of the coming of a steamer, and his mind was busy with plans for entrapping the Doctor.

But, though the priest gave his entire attention to the game, he lost constantly, and finally he threw down his cards with the impatient exclamation, "I can play no longer, for I have nothing left to stake but my cassock and breviary."

Mr. Jenkins absent-mindedly drew in his winnings, and as he did so his thoughts were something like these: "I must stick close to the Doctor, but even if I find him he is not likely to desire my company, and he will give me the slip again at the first opportunity. I must get up some disguise, and make his acquaintance again under a new personality. Eh! what did you say?" he asked the priest. "You want to play for your clothes. You have another suit I suppose. Well, I don't mind. Here's what I have already won from you against a gown, a skull-cap, a prayer-book and a rosary."

Mr. Jenkins was certainly an adept in card-playing, for once again he won. The priest handed him a little bag containing his extra wardrobe, and Mr. Jenkins good-naturedly returned his other winnings. A half-hour later a strange priest, whose gaunt form was clothed in a very ill fitting and baggy gown evidently made for a person of very different proportions, strolled down to the landing, carrying a hand-bag and a sneak-box, and took passage on a steamer bound down the river.

Dr. Stillman remained for several days with his patient and had the satisfaction of seeing her gain rapidly. It was good for him to receive encouragement now in the direction of his chosen life-work, for his pride had been severely wounded and he was sorely in need of consolation.

One day, just as he was becoming convinced that his ministrations of mercy were no longer needed, the tall figure of a priest darkened the door of the poor hut, and he heard the voice of the daughter of the sick woman in altercation with the stranger. "Thanks be to the Virgin, you are not needed," she said. "You have doubtless heard that my mother was dying, but the good doctor has recovered her of her malady, and, glory be to the saints, she has no longer any need of the consolations of religion."

This was rather a strange way of putting it, the Doctor thought.

THE FALSE PRIEST.

Was it true that only when in sore trouble the human heart reaches out for God's help?

The voices continued, and the priest did not seem inclined to go away; indeed the Doctor fancied that he was asking for him, and he came forward to ascertain his business. The stranger was a spare clean-shaven man with an immense pair of wire goggles protecting his eyes. He spoke to the Doctor in English. "My name is Brother Dennis," he said. "I am an Irishman from the monastery of St. Patrick in the County Kerry. I have been sent out to this country by my superior to locate a mission. I have scanty knowledge of the language, and hearing that you were also a foreigner, travelling for pleasure, I have taken the liberty to ask you if I may profit by your company so long as our paths lie in the same direction."

There was something indefinably familiar in the stranger's voice. It seemed to the Doctor that he must have met him before, but he could not remember ever to have seen just such a person. His good impulses prompted him to be of what service he could, and he informed Brother Dennis that he was now ready to ascend the river and would be glad of his companionship. Brother Dennis proved an entertaining comrade; he talked much, and he had an insinuating manner which led the Doctor to unbosom much of his own private history. He drew a well-thumbed pack of cards from the pocket of his gown on their first day together on board the steamer, and was greatly disappointed to find that the Doctor did not play. He seemed to have a good deal of luggage for a travelling Dominican, but probably that great brown-paper parcel was filled with religious books for distribution among the natives. When apparently engaged in reading his breviary he watched the Doctor closely, and soon discovered that there was a secret preying upon his mind. As they sat on deck in the moonlight the second evening, Brother Dennis, who had become very intimate for their brief acquaintance, began to speak of the relief of mind afforded by the Roman Catholic religion by the confessional. "Ah! my friend," he exclaimed, "imagine the torture of a convicting conscience silenced forever, the pangs of remorse obliterated in the peace of absolution, and your secret safely guarded in the bosom of the church."

He spoke long and glowingly in this strain, without awakening any response from his companion, who admitted, indeed, that he was unhappy, but assured him that he saw no allurements in confession.

"You are a sly one," the false priest said to himself; "but I will find out your secret for all your pains to conceal it."

Mr. Jenkins was sure that the funds stolen from Gold, Glitter & Co., which were principally in coin and bills of exchange on foreign houses, must be safely stored somewhere in the Doctor's baggage. He searched everything carefully as he found opportunity, boring through the sides and bottom of the medicine chest with a fine gimlet, without finding any secret compartments. There was rather too expensive a set of surgical instruments to have been provided simply as bits of theatrical property and make-up, and the Doctor read certain abstruse medical works with a greater gusto than Father Dennis bestowed upon his breviary. "What if I am a fool after all?" he said to himself. "Some one else will get that five thousand dollars, and I shall be the laughing-stock of the entire detective force."

But Dr. Stillman spent much of his time lately in writing. Sometimes he appeared to give great thought to what he wrote, and the page grew only by a line or two in as many hours; again he would dash off sheet after sheet with the energy of inspiration, but after he had written for a long time he would invariably tear up what he had composed and scatter it upon the river in a hundred tiny bits; then he would spring from his seat and excitedly pace the deck, while Mr. Jenkins, *alias* Brother Dennis, sat and watched him, drawing his own conclusions. What could he be writing,—a medical thesis? Mr. Jenkins did not think so, and he was determined that when the letter, or whatever it might prove to be, was finished, Brother Dennis should be its first reader. Meantime, where could he conceal the stolen funds? The conclusion was inevitable that they must be about his person. At their last landing before reaching Santarem the Doctor indulged in a swim. Mr. Jenkins watched him turn into a little creek, and then made a hurried but thorough examination of his clothing, carefully searching for false pockets and double linings without anything in the least suspicious.

At Santarem the Doctor had informed him that he had business,—

CANOEING IN A SUBMERGED FOREST.

"probably," Mr. Jenkins thought, "the investment of some of his ill-gotten gains," and here he determined to redouble his vigilance.

The Doctor's first errand at Santarem was to inquire whether there were any letters awaiting him. He was handed a short one from the

Professor, announcing the arrival of his party and their acceptance of an invitation to visit the fazenda of a certain Senhor Palacios. The Doctor made inquiries as to the situation of this fazenda and engaged a boatman to take him up the Tapajos. He did not invite Brother Dennis to accompany him; but a second canoe followed the Doctor's as it turned into the Tapajos.

CHAPTER IX.

A JAGUAR HUNT.

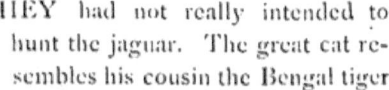

THEY had not really intended to hunt the jaguar. The great cat resembles his cousin the Bengal tiger too strongly for the girls to have any longing for his acquaintance. But the Senhor had proposed that they should go into the forest for a two days' hunt, hoping to bring back a fine collection of birds.

Beyond his cane-fields there was an old wagon-track leading like a tunnel into the heart of the wood. It was the trail of a party of surveyors. The Indians of the fazenda had kept it pretty clear of under-brush on their hunting expeditions, finding it the easiest way of penetrating the forest. They reported a spring and a good place for camping at a distance of twenty miles, and the Senhor gave the order to harness four mules to a lumbering cart, the only conveyance on the premises.

"I shall import a carriage from the States," he informs Victoria, "when my sister comes to keep house for me." He is continually confiding to Victoria his plans of what he intends to do when his sister comes, and asking her advice about everything. He will lay out a carriage-drive here; and will she oblige him by making a plan of what she would consider a model country-house, or manor,— something in the French chateau style, and more extensive than a villa. Women should be the architects, for houses are built for them, and in this project expense is not to be in the least considered. Victoria is pleased and flattered, and enters with lively interest into the scheme.

The Senhor, with his guests and a half dozen servants, among whom were Graciliano and Pedro, started on their camping excursion, while the other inhabitants of the plantation gathered to see them off, staring adults as well as children, in wide-eyed admiration and simple wonder.

Fortune was certainly on the Senhor's side, for he could not have managed his departure more opportunely had he known that an hour later the

SEEING THEM OFF.

Doctor's canoe would have reached the sawmill. He was in high spirits, and chatted of the game that they would bring back,— plenty of toothsome pacas, small animals resembling rabbits,— and even promised the girls a shot at the red deer which sometimes come down to the forest spring to drink. Pedro said the forest was alive with howling monkeys, and that he had found there magnificent hyacinthine macaws. The Professor took his butterfly-net, and at last all were ready; the girls and the Professor rode on the top of the cart, the Senhor guided his hard-mouthed four-in-hand with Victoria at his side on the high spring seat. Two of the men went on in advance

PEDRO.

with axes to clear the way of *cipos*, or long, looping vines, and the other four trudged beside them an imposing body-guard, with their rifles over their shoulders. The girls had been practising target-shooting for several days past with pistols. It was no new accomplishment to Victoria, and she was the most expert. They left the bright and open canefield, and entered the mysterious forest, and all conversation ceased for the moment. The dusk was very impressive, only here and there flickering spots of light broke through the leafy canopy of green. There was not much foliage about them, but everywhere colonnades of aspiring treetrunks, slender or great, all struggling upward to the light. Some of them were columnar palms, some were the white chestnuts, or Brazil nut trees. Here were trees with huge, buttressed trunks, and others with stilt-like roots while the

THE PROFESSOR AT WORK.

long, straight air-roots of the aroideæ swayed like ropes from the

A GIANT OF THE FOREST.

rigging of a ship. The cipos and lianas rollicked over all, tangling and knotting everything in their snake-like convolutions. Indeed, it was difficult to tell them from snakes. Maud poked at one twisted creeper that was striped curiously, and saw it slip away from before her eyes, — it was a serpent, and a large one. So they bounced and rattled on, seeing very little in the way of life, and struck by the silence of the forest; not a note of a bird or the cry of a wild animal to be heard. But Graciliano stooped and carefully examined the tracks of some creature on the swampy ground. "*Onça?*" (jaguars?) Philomena cried inquiringly.

Graciliano was of the opinion that it was only a great ant-eater. "Good!" ejaculated the Professor; "he is an excellent pioneer, and will clear the way for us."

And then the conversation took a zoological turn, and they talked of animals and chiefly of dangerous ones. The Senhor told of an old boa-constrictor and her brood which he found living under the tiles of his house. The former owner would not dislodge him, as they kept the premises free from bats.

"I believe the true reason that he did not hunt them out," said the Senhor, " was because he was too lazy. It needed a little Yankee enterprise and that I brought."

"But you are not a Yankee," Maud replied dryly.

"Certainly not, but I brought back from the States a good many Yankee inventions, and I pride myself that energy is one of them." The Senhor said this unconcernedly enough, but he bit his lip before he spoke and regarded Maud stealthily from the corner of his eye, as though calculating the effect of the remark upon her. That young lady was looking studiously at Victoria, but she made her next remark with the explosiveness of a pistol-shot.

"Senhor Silva, you are not in the least like a Brazilian."

"Indeed! with what Brazilian have you done me the honor to compare me?"

Maud hesitated; she was not acquainted with a single native of Brazil, and she saw her mistake. "I ought to have said that you are very like a Yankee."

"We are all sons and daughters of Adam, and not so very unlike after all."

"The study of ethnology is a very interesting one," began the Professor. But he was not allowed to continue his remarks, for Victoria wanted to know if really any jaguars had been seen near the fazenda lately. Graciliano was questioned, and replied that he had seen one fishing on the Tapajos the day before their excursion.

Victoria laughed derisively. "That is quite equal to his stories of the dolphin," she said; "does he want us to believe that the jaguars go out in canoes, with firebrands and tridents, to spear fish?"

"No," replied the Senhor. "But Graciliano is really in earnest, and I think correct in his statement. The jaguar will lie close to the water on some overhanging branch, and gently lash the surface with his tail. The splash sounds like the fall of ripe fruit, and a fish frequently rises and is caught by the jaguar's sharp claws."

"What a cunning creature he must be," said Delight. "I wonder if Philomena cannot tell us some Indian stories about him. She entertained us for a long time last evening with tales that were very much like Uncle Remus's stories of Brer Fox and Brer Rabbit."

"Philomena must be induced to favor us," Victoria said, "for my knowledge of jaguar literature is remarkably limited, it is entirely confined in fact to the touching ballad of the Old Woman of Nicaragua."

"What is that?" the Senhor asked.

"Have you never heard? —

> 'There was an old woman of Nicaragua
> Whose back hair was clawed off by a jaguar.
> The old woman said, Ah!
> The jaguar said, Bah!
> What a false, artificial old hag you are!'"

JAGUAR FISHING.

All laughed, and Philomena, on being questioned, replied that the Indians called the jaguar the son of Jurupary, — child of the devil. He was very fierce and strong, but the *cotia* sometimes outwitted him.

"Mr. Herbert Smith brought back a number of those South American folk-lore stories," said the Professor. "I remember he reports the Indian explanation of how the tortoise came by his shell."

"Let Philomena tell it," Delight begged.

"The tortoise at first had no shell," said Philomena, "but a jaguar bit into its back so fiercely that its teeth locked together, and it could not get them apart. Then the jaguar died and the tortoise running through the forest tore its head from its body. Finally nothing remained but the skull bleached by the weather, and the tortoise wears the jaguar's skull on its back to this day."

"That is very interesting," said Victoria, "please tell us some more."

"The cotia," said Philomena, "is a very wise and also a very mischievous little animal. One day the jaguar said to him, 'O Cotia, I am going to marry the King Deer's daughter.' Then the cotia went to the deer and said, 'O King Deer, the jaguar, for all he is so big, is a coward and I can ride him.' 'Do so,' said the deer, 'and I will break my word to him, and you shall marry my daughter.' Then the cotia waited at a little distance from the deer's fazenda for the coming of the jaguar. When he came, the cotia said, in a very weak voice, 'I am ill; carry me home, good, kind jaguar.' And the jaguar took pity on him, and allowed him to mount upon his back. But when they reached the King Deer's fazenda the cotia sat up very straight, and dug his heels into the jaguar's ribs, and began to lash him with a cipo which he held in his paw. Then the jaguar was angry, and rushed by very fast, trying to throw the cotia off, and the cotia caught hold of a hanging vine and escaped among the branches of the tree. When the jaguar found how he had been fooled, he determined to kill the cotia. Now there was only one spring in the forest, and he knew if he lay in wait here the cotia must come, sooner or later, to drink. Now the cotia knew that the jaguar was lying in wait for him at the spring, and kept away until he became very thirsty. Then he saw an old woman going through the forest with a jar on her head. He ran before her and lay in her path, feigning to be dead. She pushed him out of the way with her foot, saying, 'One dead cotia is not worth picking up.' The cotia waited until the

THE DRIED LEAVES ANIMAL.

woman had gone on, then he got up, ran on ahead, and again feigned himself dead. The woman then said, 'Even two dead cotias are not worth picking up.' The cotia repeated the trick a third time and the woman now said, 'One dead cotia is not worth picking up, neither are two, but three are. I will go back for the other two and leave this one beside my jar until I return.' As soon as she was out of sight the cotia overturned the jar, but to his disappointment found that it contained molasses instead of water. However, he determined to make the best of it, and rolled himself first in the molasses, and then in a bed of dried leaves. This he repeated several times, until his appearance was quite changed. He then went boldly to the spring. The jaguar challenged him crying out 'Whom have we here?' 'I am the dried-leaves animal,' the cotia replied, and the jaguar allowed him to drink and go away.

"Afterward, when he heard that he had been tricked again, the jaguar retired to his den and gave out that he was dead. 'The cotia will come to look at my body,' he thought. All the beasts of the forest collected around the mouth of the den and looked in. 'He is really dead,' they said. The cotia came last of all. 'Has he groaned three times?' he asked. 'When my grandmother died she groaned three times.'

"The jaguar, hearing this, groaned three times. The cotia laughed and ran away, saying, 'Dead jaguars do not groan.'"

Philomena had finished her recital for that time, but after this it was never difficult to coax her to a story, and many and curious were the fables which she told. Better than Æsop, the girls thought, for there was never a *Hæc fabula docet* at the end. Some way, to Maud's mind, the fable had its application after all. This wily handsome Senhor was the jaguar. Victoria, slender and graceful, was the fawn, the King Deer's daughter. Maud was only an insignificant member of the company as yet, but might she not outwit her jaguar as cleverly as the cotia had done?

They picnicked at noon and soon after reached their camping ground. A tent was pitched with six hammocks radiating from the central pole, to serve as dormitory for Mrs. Holmes, the girls, and their maid. The camp-fire was built in front of this tent, and, opposite, the hammocks of the men were hung from tree to tree. Behind the girls' tent the ground sloped to the spring, and all around their little clearing the forest shut them in with its almost impassable palisade. Toward night the howling of the monkeys began; an indescribably doleful sound. The smoke of the camp-fire drove away the mosquitoes, and they sat late about it, listening to and telling stories. "Let us have a song before we retire," said the Professor, and the Senhor brought out a guitar, and sang to a little jingling accompaniment an Indian song, whose translation Mr. Herbert Smith also gives in his "Brazil, the Amazons, and the Coast."

> "I swung in my drowsy hammock,
>   And wooed the forest boughs,
> But they answered low 'There's pain and woe
>   In the lovers' foolish vows.'
>
> "Little fish in the deep, dark pool,
>   Fickle sand of the sea,
> How can I ever love you alone,
>   Since you will not alone love me?
>
> "What if I drift away, away,
>   Alone on the ocean swell;
> What if I die with no one nigh
>   Of the friends who love me well?
>
> "Yet I have the sun for my lover true,
>   The moon for my lady bright,—
> The sun to walk with alone all day,
>   The moon in the silent night."

After retiring, Maud lay awake a long time trying to analyze her distrust for the Senhor. Everyone else seemed fascinated with him, why should she perversely refuse her good opinion. In the first place, he was fastidious, a creature almost

> "Too fine and good
> For human nature's daily food."

He had a habit of fault-finding with his servants, which seemed to indicate a petty, dictatorial nature, and to hint that his obsequious

A HALT IN THE FOREST.

politeness was only a thin veneer over a great selfishness. Ah! there was the word. She had found the keynote of his character,—the Senhor was supremely and unscrupulously selfish. She felt that he would hesitate at almost no step which would advance his personal comfort or ambition. This was told by a hundred little things, by a word let drop now and then, by a mere shrug of the shoulders, or a thoughtless act. The man was bound up in self. If he had treated them kindly Maud was sure it was only because he had some interest at stake, and that interest was evidently Victoria. "If he really loved her," Maud thought, "that would be something to respect him for; but I do not believe he is capable of true love. If a jaguar were to spring at her he would run away, and leave her to her fate."

At this point in Maud's reverie Victoria arose, and, parting the tent curtains, looked out. She returned a moment later, and, seeing that Maud was awake, spoke. "It is a glorious moonlight night, and it's of no use trying, I cannot sleep. The Senhor is pacing up and down outside, guarding our tent. Is it not romantic?"

"Very," replied Maud dryly, "probably the mosquitoes will not let him sleep."

"I am desperately thirsty, where is the water-cooler?"

"By the tent-pole."

Victoria lifted it to her lips and was about to drink when she noticed some one had left it open, and a lizard had crept inside. She emptied the urn with an expression of disgust. "Never mind," she added, "it is only a step to the spring, and I must have some water."

"Victoria," Maud called after her, "you surely are not going down there alone," but the fearless girl had gone. The Senhor, hearing the voices, rapped at the tent and asked if all was right.

"Victoria has just gone to the spring," Maud replied. "I wish you would look after her," and the Senhor caught his gun and followed her in a twinkling. The spring was near, and when Victoria stepped from the tent she saw it shining before her in the moonlight like a silver mirror. The path was clearly outlined, and yet an undefined dread made her hesitate an instant: it was only an instant, however, and she then ran nimbly down the little terrace and stooped to fill her earthen water-cooler. Just then there was a crackling of branches, and, raising her head, she saw two fiery eyes glowering at her from across the spring, and an undefined form crouching in the darkness. She was a brave girl and she did not realize her peril. "It is some timid creature of the woods," she thought, and she waved the urn in her hand, stamped her foot, and cried, "Shoo!" The creature responded by a savage growl, and she could see it lashing its tail from side to side. Then the thought came to her that this was a jaguar, and she felt herself growing faint with fright, but a steady voice behind her said, "Don't move"—a ringing shot pealed through the air from just over her shoulder, and, with a bound such as a cat will give, the jaguar leaped into the air, and fell dead at her feet. She was splashed with water, for the animal had fallen partly into the spring,

"A RINGING SHOT PEALED THROUGH THE AIR."

and the cold dash in her face helped to restore her, and enabled her to say with self possession, though her face was still very white, — "You have saved my life; I thank you."

"You are welcome," replied the Senhor, with lips which trembled: "but never do such a foolish thing again. Your life is too precious to me; you have no right to peril it."

"I will not," Victoria replied, quite humbly, and by this time the whole camp was with them, the men with their guns and firebrands, the girls standing in the looped-back tent, peering anxiously into the darkness. The Senhor handed Victoria back to them, and the men brought the jaguar around to the fire, but not until they had fired several shots into his body. He was a huge creature, with a tawny skin marked with black "roses," — circles of curved lines with a dot in the centre. Graciliano declared that it was the very creature whom he had seen fishing, and which had carried away a calf from the cattle fazenda of their neighbor who supplied Santarem with milk. The Senhor ordered the men to skin the creature carefully, as he wished a rug made of it for the Senhorita.

"I wronged him after all," thought Maud; "whatever his faults may be, he is not a coward."

Victoria, now that the excitement was over, was quite unstrung. She sat in Delight's hammock, with her arms around her friend's neck, weeping from sheer nervousness. Suddenly her weeping changed to hysterical laughter.

"Control yourself, you absurd child," Maud exclaimed, "or they will all think you have gone crazy." But Victoria could not stop for several minutes.

"O Maud," she said at length, "it was dreadful, and yet it had its grotesque side, too. He was as mad at me as he could be, and he scolded me like a schoolmaster, as he had a perfect right, for of course, it was a reckless thing to do; but, O girls! he did look so ridiculous. — his eyes popping out of his head, his face as white as chalk, and his wig all on one side, for all the world like the old woman of Nicaragua."

"His wig!" exclaimed both of the girls in unison.

"Yes, dears, he wears a wig. What a fraud he is! He must be as old as the Professor. It was all I could do to forbear exclaiming, 'What a false, artificial old hag you are!'"

CHAPTER X.

VICTORIA REGIA.

KILLING the jaguar was glory and adventure enough, and the party returned to the fazenda early the next day, contenting themselves with only a few birds and a monkey or two. Their return was hastened by the Professor's not feeling quite well.

"I fear," said the Senhor, "that he is going to have a touch of the ague. Camping out is not just the thing for a man of his age."

Victoria threw an arch glance at Delight and bit her lip. But Delight hardly noticed it, she was really anxious about her father, and Mrs. Holmes was equally impatient to return to the fazenda. "If that obliging Dr. Stillman were only within call," she said, and meantime Dr. Stillman was not only quite within reach if they had but known it, but was impatiently waiting some communication from them at Santarem. On the morning of his visit at the fazenda, disappointed by the information that his friends had left, no one knew exactly in what direction, for a stay of uncertain duration, he had wandered irresolutely about the place, and had finally accepted the steward's invitation to step into the Senhor's office and leave a written message. Under the pressure of the sudden opportunity he wrote the letter which he had so often written and destroyed on his voyage up the river. It was humble enough to have pleased even Victoria's haughty disposition. He craved her forgiveness for any possible offence, and he told her of his love in manly terms that would have commanded her respect had the letter ever met her eye. "I was too hasty at Breves," he said, "and I will wait at Santarem for your answer."

As he stepped into his canoe he noticed a second one moored beside it, but he did not see the lynx face of Brother Dennis watching him from behind a pile of lumber. As soon as the Doctor was well out of sight, Brother Dennis entered the Senhor's office and saw the letter addressed to Victoria lying upon the desk. He unscrupulously opened the same. As he perused the pages the doubt as to his own sagacity gradually deepened. If the Doctor were really a defaulter, loaded with immense wealth, he would not have told this aristocratic heiress that in point of worldly possessions he was immeasurably her inferior; that he had nothing but his profession, and an opening promised him in one of the New York hospitals. His references to his family, and indeed the whole tone of his letter, were proofs positive of his innocence. "I am off the track," muttered Mr. Jenkins, "sold for once, and the proceeds uncollectible." He carefully resealed the letter so that it should show no trace of having been tampered with, and embarked for Santarem, his forehead seamed with wrinkles which betokened deep thought.

"Since Doctor Stillman is not the man," he said to himself, "I must investigate that Senhor Silva. But the puzzle is where to find him." It never occurred to the astute Mr. Jenkins that Senhor Palacios, whose estate he had just visited, could be the man he sought. "He told the young ladies that he was going up the river, and he is pretty likely to turn up somewhere in their path. My best plan will be to follow them." Brother Dennis accordingly also established himself at Santarem, waiting the departure of the Professor and his party.

On his return from the woods the Senhor naturally looked over the few letters which had arrived during his absence. The one addressed to Victoria caught his eye, and a second time it was opened and read by other eyes than those for whom it was intended. But the Senhor, having read and disapproved of the contents, did not reseal the letter as Mr. Jenkins had done. He carefully destroyed it in the same way in which he had served Maud's letter to her Lisbon friend. He did even more. He answered the letter. He judged correctly that the Doctor was not familiar with Victoria's hand and he could safely venture so far. He phrased the letter curtly and formally, and could not forbear adding a venomed allusion to his poverty which Victoria herself could never have made. This letter accomplished its mission. The Doctor accepted it as final, and embarked on a boat going up the river, not that he cared in the least in what direction he went, but because it was the first boat which happened to touch Santarem. Brother Dennis did not accompany him, he had other fish to fry.

THE SENHOR READS AND DISAPPROVES.

Toasting, rubbing, and dosing under Mrs. Holmes's hands soon restored the Professor, and in a day or two the old gentleman was as lively as ever, and possessed with his old restlessness to be off and away on his expedition. The Senhor and he had long arguments as to the comparative merits of the upper Tapajos and the Madeira. The Professor was interested in the Madeira and Mamoré Railroad, which was intended to open up Bolivia to commerce, by circling the rapids and falls which for two hundred and thirty miles obstruct navigation on the Madeira. He wished to go over this ground carefully, expecting to find many new fossils, and opportunity to study geologic conformation in the cuts made by the railroad, and to push on to the old mission of Exaltacion in Bolivia, from whence it was his ambitious project to circle Lake Titicaca, then Cuzco, with a study of the Incas, and across the Andes to the coast, which they would follow up to Panama in easy stages on the Pacific Mail steamers.

The Senhor objected that this trip would be too adventurous and fatiguing for the ladies, and even for the Professor himself, and urged a substitution of the thorough exploration of the Tapajos and its tributaries, for which purpose he offered his little steamer, which would soon arrive from its wooding expedition. "The Tapajos," he said, "leads to the Matto Grosso and the diamond district. At Itaituba we can leave the steamer and take to canoes as far as Diamantina. I will take my own canoes and paddlers with me, so that we will not have to depend on obtaining chance labor. From Diamantina it will be easy to make a portage to the Paraguay, which we can descend in our canoes until I can place you on board some good steamer bound down the La Plata to Monte Video, from which point you can readily obtain passage for New York."

"Your plan is a tempting one, my dear Senhor," replied the Professor, "but I cannot allow you to be at so much trouble and expense on our behalf."

"It is entirely on my own behalf," the Senhor replied. "I contemplate making just such a trip for the furtherance of my own business. I trust you will allow me to carry out a plan I have already formed, and which I only hope will prove as advantageous to you as I am sure it will be for me."

Mrs. Holmes, always careful of the Professor's comfort, reminded her husband that this journey would contain fewer risks, while it would take them over a much wider extent of country than the one which he had marked out for himself, and would furnish as likely a field for marine fossils as the Madeira.

"You must put it to vote," said the Senhor, with easy confidence; "but first, allow me to bribe the voters. I promise a handsome solitaire from the diamond district to every one who favors my plan. Come, who is for the Madeira, now, with its fevers and hardships?"

Maud raised her hand with quiet determination, and the Professor, protesting his thanks, still persisted in his former determination.

Mrs. Holmes and Delight voted for accepting the Senhor's offer, while Victoria declined to express a preference.

"Will you not give the decisive vote, Miss Delavan?" the Senhor pleaded; but Victoria shook her head in demure perverseness.

"It is just a tie as it stands," said the Senhor gayly, "and of course that means that you do not go away at all. You must stay here until you can come to an unanimous decision, and with that arrangement I am more than satisfied. To-morrow we will take to the canoes and follow up an *igaripé* to a lake that Graciliano tells me of, where grow some remarkably fine specimens of that queen of water-lilies, the Victoria Regia."

This excursion proved to be the climax of their visit. All their other experiences seemed only to lead up to it. The party set out in small canoes, threading the igaripés (little lakes and navigable marshes), over which the palms, fig-trees, tree ferns, bananas, and other tropical foliage, matted their green canopies, and "lithe lianas starred with flowers, hung like strung jewels." There were occasional portages, where there was hard pushing and tugging for the Indians to transfer the boats from one canoe path to another, and where the girls were carried in hammocks across the marshy ground by two sturdy Indian bearers. "I feel like a Hindoo princess in my sedan chair," Victoria announced gayly to the Professor, who passed her mounted pick-a-back on Graciliano's brawny shoulders, the short legs of the Indian sinking to the knees in the mire, and the longer ones of the Professor, with all their twisting, nearly reaching the surface of the marsh. They found more birds on this excursion than on any other, — gem-like humming-birds, with throats of emerald and topaz, royal ruby or amethyst; a macaw swept her violet train through the pillared aisles like an empress moving through some cathedral to her coronation, while a flamingo stalked through the choir of foliage, a cardinal assisting at the ceremony. This was Victoria's fancy, and voted a pretty one, while Maud compared a gorgeous parrot to a courtier of the time of the *Grand Monarque*, flashing in embroidered satin and brocade. Butterflies of every color fluttered about them,—"swallow-tailed papilios, green, rose, violet, and black,"— and the king of all the butterfly race, the magnificent blue butterfly of the Amazons. It seemed to Victoria that she was under the influence of a spell, and had been ever since her arrival at the fazenda. It was here that the full fascination of this tropical land had been poured upon her — all its luxury concentrated and its hardships weeded out. Darwin called the country "one great, wild, untidy, luxuriant hot-house," and it seemed to her that this conservatory gone wild was the work of a powerful enchanter, and might vanish at the touch of his magic wand. Without doubt the Senhor

THE PROFESSOR BOTANIZING.

was an enchanter, and whatever may have been his power over nature about her, he was beginning to exercise a decided influence over Victoria herself. Victoria realized this, and it troubled her. When the decision of the itinerary was referred to her, her inclination spoke at once in favor of the Paraguay and a continuation of this pleasant acquaintance, but her better judgment also spoke within her,—"Better break off this association before it becomes indispensable;" and she held herself and the Senhor in grave scrutiny. Before starting on this last trip she had made Maud promise to take her usual place in the Senhor's canoe, as she preferred Delight's company, and, exclusive of the paddlers, there would be only room for two in each of these smaller boats.

TROPICAL FOLIAGE.

Maud had taken a sort of grim pleasure in the request. "How vexed he will be," she thought, "and how I shall enjoy his vexation," but when the party started, the Senhor, actuated by some unaccountable whim, invited her of his own accord to a seat in his canoe.

The girls looked at each other somewhat blankly, and Maud took her place chagrined, and half inclined to refuse the invitation. The Senhor's boat shot ahead, keeping the lead all the way, and the Senhor could not have exerted himself more to please Victoria than he did to gain Maud's good will. But Maud, to use her own expression, was "grumpy," and not to be pleased. Suddenly the Senhor looked her steadily in the face, and asked, "What have I done, Miss Van Vechten, to merit your ill opinion?"

Was it simple frankness or the height of effrontery? To Maud

MACAWS.

it seemed the latter, and she replied stiffly that she was sorry if she had been so deficient in good breeding as to treat so polite a host with rudeness.

"Never mind politeness for the moment," the Senhor remarked blandly, "let us be perfectly sincere. You distrust me. Why is it?"

Maud was driven into a corner and replied recklessly, "Perhaps it is because I am constructed something on the principle of the armadillo. My heart is pretty effectually encased in armor, and it would be hard for anyone to touch it."

"Is it true, then," asked the Senhor, "as I have read, that an

American girl of the North has 'the head of a railway president and the heart of an Esquimaux.'"

"The author who wrote that did not intend to compliment us, but if it is true, as I imagine, that Esquimaux have very simple, kindly hearts, like other people, and railway presidents are only shrewd and honest calculators of the results of every venture before they allow themselves to be interested in it, then I believe the comparison is a just one."

"And you have gone through a very exact mathematical calculation and have decided that I am a poor investment."

"How preposterous," Maud exclaimed. "Of what possible concern of mine can your character be?"

"What a clear head you have," the Senhor replied with a significant smile, "and how well you put things. You have divined the truth that I am deeply interested in your friend, and, though you have a prejudice against me yourself, you acknowledge that it is no affair of yours, and your innate love of justice will not allow you to interfere to influence her. You have really a most extraordinary character and one that commands my utmost respect."

Maud bit her lip with vexation. "I did not intend to promise that I would not interfere if I saw any real cause for doing so," she said.

"But until you have something against me more tangible than your own aversion you will not influence her."

"I think you overestimate my influence; we are not very intimate. Delight is her confidential friend, and she believes in you most thoroughly."

"Thank her for that. I wish I could convince you also of my integrity."

"I wish you would not talk so, Senhor Palacios. I have nothing against you, and you may rest quite easy I will not take the field as your antagonist until I have."

The Senhor bowed gayly, and just then they reached their last portage. Maud and Victoria found themselves side by side for a moment, and Maud whispered, "You must really change places with me, I have had quite enough of that man."

The transfer was effected pleasantly, and presently the boats drifted into the placid waters of the lily lake. The surface was spotted with the huge lily pads, saucer-shaped, a rich green on the upper surface, with upturned edges showing the crimson lining, some of them eight feet across. The Indians call these enormous saucers *fornos*, or braziers. Over these anchored rafts fleet-footed little *jacanas*, or ramrod chickens, a bird akin to the sandpiper, ran races among the buds and flowers. And such flowers! larger than our largest sunflowers,— some of them

"I HAVE HAD QUITE ENOUGH OF THAT MAN."

eighteen inches across, great carven blossoms, a bouquet of our pond-lilies in a single flower. Pure and white, the bud opens slowly, the petals separating as the day advances, until, in its majestic loveliness, it has attained its full size. This is the lily when a day old; on the second day they have outlived their snowy innocence, and are all one blush of exquisite pink, with a centre of bright yellow. Three days completes the life of the Victoria Regia, and on the third the queen lily is arrayed in royal purple; but she wears it with a world-weary languor, as though, like the great Sultan Solomon, she had tasted of every sweet in life and had found all vanity. Out on the lake this process is going on all the time; buds, flowers, white, pink, and purple, are displayed in every degree of perfection. The Indians sprang into the water and began the difficult task of cutting the leathery and spiny stalks, and of uprooting plants, which the Senhor designed to transplant to the fazenda. Some of these leaves are so strongly built and strengthened by interlacing braces that they will support a young child. The boats were laden with a fragrant freight, and once more

VICTORIA REGIA.

they threaded the labyrinthine igaripé, but this time Victoria and the Senhor were together, and he urged her to give the casting vote in favor of the exploration of the Tapajos. "But first," he asked, "is there anything more in the vicinity which you would like to see? With the exception of one ceremonious dinner at the Baron's and the lunch which I gave in return, you have seen nothing of Brazilian society."

"Nor do I care to," Victoria replied; "but there is one place at Santarem which I would like to visit, — the leper asylum."

The Senhor shuddered. "It would not be permitted," he said, "Whatever put the notion of that horrible place into your head?"

"Dr. Stillman visited it."

"Ah! the notion is worthy of him. The man is loathsome to me. I do not see how the Professor can endure him, or Mrs. Holmes could ever have admitted him to the society of the young ladies she was chaperoning."

"What is your objection to the Doctor?" Victoria inquired, in wide-eyed surprise.

"It is ungenerous to mention suspicions, but did you know that the photographer we saw on board ship was really not a professional photographer at all, but a detective in disguise?"

"Well, what of that?"

"I have reason to think, from information that I received before leaving the States, that Doctor Stillman was the man of whom he was in search."

"Then you should have given that information to Mr. Jenkins."

"I think I did put him on the track."

"I am sorry," Victoria said simply, "I do not believe he is the criminal, and it must be very disagreeable to be suspected."

The Senhor shrugged his shoulders. Not long after they came in sight of the fazenda. Very beautiful it looked with the tropical sunset flooding the Javary palms and the quivering plumes of the Assais.

"Was there ever a region so surpassingly lovely?" Victoria exclaimed with enthusiasm.

"Can you not imagine yourself a part of it, the Victoria Regia of this little kingdom?" the Senhor asked in a low voice.

"No," Victoria replied, apparently not comprehending his full meaning. "It is a paradise indeed, but life in such a paradise would be pure selfishness; for surely we are placed in this world to help lift up our fellow creatures and reform society, and not to desert our own country and time with its calls for earnest labor."

It was a strange speech for Victoria to make. It sounded exactly like one of the Doctor's, and she remembered with a blush that the words which had incensed her so highly and had led to their quarrel were almost identical with these. Was she coming to agree with him so exactly?

Had the Senhor known how deeply her mind was becoming interested in new aims for higher living, he might have argued that here was a mission field in the uplifting of the little community over which he reigned almost as a feudal lord. But the Senhor had no sympathy with such ideas, and he continued to press considerations of a more selfish nature. "I hope," he said, "to build here a domain. I shall add to my land and my servants until I am the most powerful proprietor in this region. I shall build a castle here which you must help me plan, and whose appointments you shall select in Europe. My family is influentially connected, and with my means it will not be difficult to purchase a title. Say that you will accept that of the Baroness da Silva y Palacios and I will secure it for you. I do not ask you to answer me now, only to think of it, and to tell me when the trip is over."

"I ought not to let you think of it as possible," Victoria said. "I ought to tell you now, once for all."

"No," he interrupted. "I will not receive my answer now; you must have time to think."

"Very well," she replied, "perhaps it will be best so."

That evening after dinner the vote was taken. The Senhor was elated and confident as he passed his wide Panama hat, but his expression changed as he read the slips, — there were only two marked Tapajos, while there were three ballots for the Madeira.

As she bade him good-night, Victoria lingered an instant behind the rest. "I can decide better away from you," she said.

"One moment, Victoria," the Senhor replied; but she had gone. "She is afraid that she will consent," the Senhor said to himself. "The battle is more than half won,"—and then he scowled deeply—"but I cannot go to the States for her. I might, however, meet her in Europe. No, that is too problematical. They must return this way, and, little as they have it in their minds, they shall do so."

CHAPTER XI.

THE MADEIRA TROUBLE.

THEIR last day at the fazenda was a busy one. The Senhor drew Maud aside early in the morning. "I would like to consult you," he said in the flattering tone in which he had latterly tried to ingratiate himself in Maud's good opinion. "I wish to make Miss Delavan a good-by present: what do you think would please her most?"

"Will you act on my suggestion?" Maud asked, "in case I give my opinion."

"Most certainly," the Senhor replied blandly.

"Then if you will sit to me for your portrait, I will do my best to make one which will keep you in her remembrance."

The Senhor shot a keen look at Maud's impenetrable face, reflected a moment, and accepted the offer. "But what can you do in one day?" he asked.

"It will only be a sketch, but I will work fast, and do my best."

Maud kept her promise and speedily washed in a striking likeness. While the painting was progressing Victoria had kept her room. "The time has come for me to write that apology to the Doctor," she said to Delight. "I wish I could see him and talk it out; however 'what must be, must,'" and Victoria wrote a gentle, lady-like note, as unlike the one which the Doctor had just received, and purporting to come from her, as sweetness from poison. This note she left with her own hands the next day at Senhor Correa's. A shabby priest was lounging in the store, and when she left he threw away the cigarette which he had been smoking and spoke to Senhor Correa. "That letter is for my friend Dr. Stillman, is it not?"

"Yes. He has gone up the river, has he not?"

"Yes. I join him by the next boat, and I will deliver it."

"Very well," and Victoria's note was safely buttoned within Brother Dennis's cassock. The priest then sauntered down to the landing and embarked on the same steamer with the Professor's party. It was doubled in size now, for the Senhor had insisted on their taking a half dozen of his own servants, among whom were Philomena Graciliano, and Pedro. "You can obtain boats easily enough up the river," he said, "but cannot always depend upon finding faithful servants."

It so happened that the Senhor could not go to Santarem to see them off, for his steamer from the upper Tapajos arrived as they were leaving, and there were a number of matters which required his immediate attention. The Indians were to return to him when they had safely conveyed the party to Exaltacion. The Senhor begged the Professor not to wait until their return, but to send him frequent news of their welfare, promising at the same time to forward letters for them to different cities on the Pacific coast, which, transferred by the usual route for crossing the continent, might be expected to reach their destination more quickly than the Professor's party.

Maud, while making her sketch of the Senhor, had noticed carefully every little peculiarity of complexion, and she had come to the conclusion that his mustache was dyed. The ends were intensely black, but close to the lip there was a little distance where it had freshly grown, where the color was much lighter. She was positive, too, that it was not gray, but a light yellow. Then she remembered Victoria's discovery in regard to the wig, and close to the Senhor's neck she discovered a curling wisp of golden hair. It was hardly long enough to be detected, a mere point shining among the glossy black waves, but Maud saw it, and it confirmed her suspicions. She had never fancied that she would long for the society of Mr. Jenkins, but she would have been greatly pleased at this juncture to have had a few moments' conversation with him, or even to have known his address. She hunted up the newspaper containing the description of Mr. Bartlett, and in the solitude of her own room that last afternoon at the fazenda she dashed in another sketch of the Senhor, following the study already made in form and feature, but changing the coloring. The effect was startling, and she was on the point of mailing the result to Messrs. Gold and Glitter, of New York, when the memory of her Lisbon friends restrained her. The brother of little Candida could not be the defaulting clerk, — and baffled and puzzled she hid the portrait in the bottom of her sketch-box.

MAUD HAS A SUSPICION.

Their voyage up the river was uneventful, — the same lazy tropical days following one upon another, the same luxuriance of tropical foliage in the landscape, and the broad yellow river flowing on to the sea. They had noticed far down toward its mouth bits of pumice-stone floating upon its surface, and every day brought them nearer the volcanoes which had sent them these hardened foam-flakes as their greetings.

Brother Dennis did not seek their society. He had succeeded in deceiving Dr. Stillman, but he wisely declined at this time to submit his disguise to the scrutiny of a bevy of sharp-eyed girls. He left them at Manaos, determined to follow them later if a clue which seemed to present itself should prove false.

The Professor availed himself of steam transportation as far as it was afforded, but found himself stranded one fine morning in a little village on the banks of the Madeira, whose principal interest consisted in its being a depot of the rubber trade. Now began the real difficulties of the trip. Two boats were hired, and the party now experienced the more arduous camp and canoe life. They carried provisions for two months, with tents, tools, medicines, and presents for the Indians whom they might meet. They mounted the river slowly, paddling against the current. The scenery was monotonous, and they passed very few settlements, even of Indians. Now and then the settlement of a Seringueiro, or the gipsy-like camp of a few Caripunas, who had come to the river in search of turtle-eggs, and everywhere else the loneliness of the wilderness. With little of outside interest they came to know each other more intimately, and Maud began to feel herself more strongly drawn to Victoria. A change had come over the girl. She was no longer careless and frivolous. She was carefully studying her own soul, and her mind was filled with a vague discontent; all her previous ambitions seemed puerile, and she longed for the "more excellent way." Delight was cheerful and merry as ever, extracting entertainment and even enthusiasm out of the most meagre material. It was Delight who first suspected a romance between Philomena and Graciliano. "He is not married at all," she informed the other girls, "as the Senhor led us to suppose, when we were talking that night about the dolphins. But he is terribly jealous of Philomena, and only came on this trip because he knew she was coming."

Delight listened to the songs which the boatmen sang, and copied them in her note-book. There was one which was so musical that Victoria learned to sing it, and her rich voice often carried the air above the supporting drone of the Indians.

> "Navigando
> En mi canoa,
> Con la proa
> Al sentenrion.
>
> Voi siguiendo
> Del Madera
> La carera
> Sin timon."

Had it not been for Delight's merry ways their interest might have palled in this long stretch of their journey, but she kept every one in good humor with her own light-heartedness.

"You remind me of a saying of Alphonse Karr," Maud remarked to her one day. "'Some people are always grumbling because roses have thorns. I am thankful that thorns have roses.'"

All went well until they reached San Antonio, the first of the eighteen falls of the Madeira. Here is a Brazilian outpost, abandoned in times past on account of fevers, and scantily garrisoned at the time of their visit with a few soldiers. San Antonio was made, as late as 1882, the depot for the railroad supplies, rolling-stock, engine, rails, houses, and other property of the Madeira and Marmori Railroad. It was sad to witness the abandonment of this enterprise, and the waste, through the long rains, of machinery and property exceeding one hundred thousand dollars in value. They were told that the road, as far as it had been cut through the forest, was so completely overgrown as to be scarcely traceable, while every particle of movable material left unguarded had been carried away by the Indians. Now began the portages which it was necessary to repeat so frequently as they proceeded. The boats were unloaded and towed up the rapids, while the packages and boxes were carried on the backs of the Indians along the shore. At the Theotino Cataract, the next considerable fall, it was necessary to transport the boats themselves on land for nearly eight hundred yards. Rollers were placed beneath them, but the process was very tedious and wearisome even for the sturdy Indians.

The scenery was no longer monotonous, but, broken by ranges of hills, it was in some places wildly picturesque. The Theotino Cataract was especially imposing. The spectacle of its whirling, tossing spray; its black crags and leaping waves playing with the driftwood and tossing tree-trunks into the air as though they were child's playthings, was exhilarating, and thrilled the nerves with a sympathetic sense of power. The portage, however, was difficult, and Maud heard the servants grumbling among themselves; Pedro apparently pacified in a sentence of which Maud could only understand the words, "Not here, but at the Caldeirao do Inferno."

The rapids of Caldeirao do Inferno, or Hell's Kettle, has the worst reputation of all the eighteen falls of the Madeira. More than one hardy traveller has been drowned in its treacherous eddies, and many a cargo has been wrecked upon its rocks. What was the consternation of the tourists, on arriving at this hazardous point, at being informed by Pedro that the Indians would go no further; that indeed this was the spot at which the Senhor had ordered them to leave the party. It was in vain that the Professor exhausted every means in his power to induce them to continue with them as far as the Mission of Exaltacion. The Indians were obdurate, and prepared one of the boats for their descent, unscrupulously lading it with food and such other articles as took their fancy. Only Philomena remained faithful. She had become strongly attached to Victoria and refused to leave her. Apparently Graciliano wasted much eloquence upon her in endeavoring to change her determination. She turned her back upon him resolutely, and he reluctantly entered the boat as it was pushed from shore. They sat down on the boxes of the Professor's fossils in utter silence; no one had a suggestion to offer, so complete was their despair. Suddenly Philomena uttered a glad cry, and pointed to the black head of a swimmer coming rapidly toward them through the water. It was Graciliano, whose resolution had deserted him, and who had returned to share the fortunes of the lady of his heart. He shook the water from him like a great Newfoundland dog, and received Philomena's joyful welcome with sheepish satisfaction.

THEOTING CATARACT.

"Tell me truly," Maud asked, "did the Senhor bid you desert us in this extremity? He promised us that you should convey us all the way to Exaltacion."

"We were not to desert you," Graciliano replied, "we were to take you back with us. The men are waiting now at the rapid of the Little Hell. If you care to return they will take you, if not, they will go back to-morrow morning without you."

"Shall we return?" Delight asked. "What other alternative have we?"

"Return to Senhor Silva's!" Victoria exclaimed. "Never."

"Not necessarily to Senhor Silva," Mrs. Holmes suggested; "but to Manaos, where we can take the steamer for Para."

"We ought to be able to hire Indian paddlers in this vicinity," the Professor suggested, "and if so, we can continue our journey as we have planned it. I do not like to trust our lives in the hands of those treacherous men again. They have stolen our goods, and, rather than convey us to a civilized region, where they would be compelled to restore them, I fear they might be tempted to murder us all."

Graciliano, when conferred with, shrugged his shoulders, and it was decided to go into camp where they were for the night. This was effected very comfortably; for their stock of provisions and comforts, though lessened, were still sufficient for their necessities.

The next morning the Professor and Graciliano started, on what appeared to be an Indian trail, in search of a village. All day long the forlorn women waited for them on the bank of the river, but night settled upon them, and the Professor did not return. Maud thought with a shudder of the fate of Madame Odonnais, and Philomena told blood-curdling stories of tribes of savage Indians, murderers and cannibals, who roved this region, and had kidnapped men not many years before. No one slept during that night. They built a bonfire and piled driftwood upon it from time to time, not knowing whether it would prove a beacon to friend or foe. Morning dawned, and Philomena prepared breakfast, but no one could eat a morsel. Toward noon a Bolivian merchant, descending the river with a train of canoes and barges, laden with hides and tallow, came down the river bank with his servants to arrange a portage around the falls. He offered to take them down the river, but this proposal was firmly declined. Mrs. Holmes begged him to send some one in search of her husband, and he agreed to do so after he had completed the transfer of his boats.

A few hours later, much to their relief, the Professor and Graciliano appeared with three friendly Caripuna Indians, whose services they had secured. The Bolivian merchant, on examination of their canoe, agreed to exchange it for one of his own convoy above the falls, thus avoiding the transport of both around the rapids. Encouraged by this piece of good fortune and by the timely arrival of reinforcements, their goods were speedily carried up the bank, and before nightfall were safely stowed in the new canoe. For a time their troubles seemed to have ended.

The Professor made valuable discoveries of fossils, and in the broad river spaces between the rapids they progressed easily, spreading two sails with which the canoe was provided, and gliding easily along before a favorable wind. But in the repeated portages, the Professor, anxious to be of help, over-exerted himself, and when the journey was nearly accomplished he was taken ill with an intermittent fever.

"It is the tertiana," said Philomena. "The falls of the Madeira are noted for it. When the railroad was being built we used to hear that a man was buried for every sleeper laid in the track."

Their trouble was increased by Mrs. Holmes's discovery that the medicine chest had been carried away by Pedro for the sake of the brandy and Jamaica ginger which it contained. Victoria's botanical studies now came to the front. With Graciliano as pioneer, to clear

CALDEIRÃO DO INFERNO.

the way before her with an axe, she made a short excursion into the forest, and returned with some of the fruit of the guaraná. Philomena prepared the paste, moulding it into the shape of the curupira, or bird of the evil eye; for without this symbolic form she was sure the drug would lose its efficacy, and under its administration the Professor for a time experienced some relief. During their marches he was now carried in a hammock, and keeping up heart as best they could, with the knowledge that they were nearing the Cachoeira das Bananeiras, the last important fall of the Madeira.

It was at the Bananeiras, however, that the last catastrophe occurred. The violent treatment which the boat had received in its battles with sharp rocks in being towed through rapids, and especially the straining and wrenching in rolling over

MOUTH OF LATERAL RIVER, MADEIRA.

the stony ground and through the obstructing underbrush had so weakened it, that when the Indians loaded it in the rapids above the falls, the shock occasioned by the fall of a heavy box of fossils, which one of the Indians dropped, proved the last straw, and the canoe went to pieces before their eyes. Fortunately, none of the party were on board, and the Indians rescued most of the provisions, but the Professor's precious collections went to the bottom like lead. The poor man gave a cry of amazed grief, and sank back in his hammock, utterly overcome.

What was to be done? Nothing but to camp once more and wait for help. They were in the neighborhood of unfriendly Indians, notorious robbers and plunderers who, were they aware of their misfortune, would take advantage of their distressed condition; but the river was the highway,

CARIPUNA INDIAN HUNTING.

BARK CANOE OF CARIPUNA INDIANS.

and it was to be hoped that some other traveller as friendly as the Bolivian merchant would appear to their relief. The Professor's fever, increased by his excitement and disappointment, assumed a more alarming type, and, to add to their discomfort, their provisions began to give out. Graciliano and the Indians fished; there was still a good supply of farina, but the canned articles had disappeared, and only one ham remained. The Caripunas had brought with them a pair of lean and mangy dogs, who cleared the remains of every meal,

INDIAN DOGS.

and, like Pharoah's lean kine, seemed none the fatter for their eating. One morning it was discovered that the ham had disappeared, and this time one of the dogs really was fat. He lay in contented idleness, winking at them sleepily with his thievish eyes. The Indian owner, unable to say a word in defence of his pet, and apparently actuated by a desire to do the fair thing, offered to kill the dog as reparation, urging that in so doing he returned the stolen meat with interest, and assuring them that dog-flesh was very good eating.

It was Delight who retailed the story to the others, and it raised the one laugh in which they indulged during their melancholy camp on the Bananeiras. The next day a number of Indian canoes passed them, going down the river, and the Caripunas left them with the full consent of their employers, for they had no longer work or provisions for them. Graciliano killed and roasted a monkey for supper, from which Philomena and he made a plentiful meal, for the others could not bring themselves to touch it, though Philomena arranged an arm as temptingly as possible, and assured her young mistress that it was very like squirrel. The guaraná seemed no longer to exert any influence over the Professor; he was delirious and raved piteously about his theories.

"To think," said Victoria bitterly, "that it is the Senhor's perfidy which has brought us to this extremity. He pretended an interest in the Professor's work, and assured us that his servants were faithful only to wreck the expedition and make it necessary for us to return to him. But, even if he had succeeded, I do not see what advantage he could have expected to reap, since we lose our good opinion of him."

"He evidently supposed that we would blame his servants," said Maud, "and he is so very plausible that if we were to return I believe he could make us all think that he had nothing whatever to do with the matter. Now, however, there seems to be no opportunity to return. Victoria used the correct word, — we are really in extremity."

"Man's extremity is God's opportunity," said Delight with a quaver in her usually joyous voice. "When things are at their very worst the next change must be for the better, and surely nothing can be much worse than this."

Poor Delight! As she spoke, Maud and Victoria looked at each other, an unspoken fear palsying their hearts. They had watched the Professor narrowly, and had seen him slipping, slipping slowly out of their hands. Mrs. Holmes was almost crazed with anxiety, only Delight would not see the awful danger and was obstinately hopeful and cheerful. It was Maud's turn to sit up with the sick man to-night, and Victoria left the cabin and walked desperately and aimlessly down to the foaming water below the fall. "If he dies," she said to herself, "what will become of us? It is true that we have plenty of money, but in our condition it is of no more use than Crusoe's gold on the uninhabited island. He must *not* die, and yet without help he surely will. Oh! where is Dr. Stillman?" In her despair she had uttered the cry aloud, thinking herself quite alone. Now to her alarm she saw a dark figure gliding along the river bank toward her. She turned and walked rapidly toward the cabin, but looking over her shoulder she saw that the man had also quickened his pace and was gaining upon her. The stories of the kidnapping Indians flashed upon her mind, and she ran frantically. She might have escaped, but the ground was rocky and uneven. She tripped on a rolling stone and fell violently forward. She tried to rise, and as she did so she felt a firm grasp upon her shoulder, and, brave girl as she was, she fainted quite away.

CHAPTER XII.

HELP.

WHEN Mr. Jenkins left the steamer he imagined himself on the track of the Senhor. A merchant bearing the name of Silva had come up the river with the Captain on a previous trip, and had stopped at Manaos. At Manaos, therefore, Mr. Jenkins disembarked and proceeded to make inquiries concerning his man, whom he found, to his disgust, to be a perfectly reputable and ancient resident of the place, a wealthy, aged, and corpulent individual, surrounded by a large family. Mr. Jenkins should not have built too much upon the name, which he now found to be as common in Brazil as its equivalent, Wood, in the United States. Before descending the river Mr. Jenkins met the Doctor, as he imagined that he might; but he scarcely recognized him, he had become so thin and dejected.

"Cheer up, my friend," he exclaimed, giving the young man a hearty blow upon the shoulder. "I have brought you an answer to the letter which you left at the sawmill on the Tapajos last week."

The Doctor received the letter with a look of wonder, and as he read it his mystification deepened. "I do not understand this, Brother Dennis," he said. "It purports to be from a lady of my acquaintance, but I have already received a letter from her, written in a very different tone and hand."

"Conclusion is evident that one of the letters is a forgery," said Mr. Jenkins cheerfully.

"Yes, but which letter? It makes worlds of difference for me."

"I saw Miss Victoria Delavan place this letter in Senhor Correa's keeping with her own hands."

"Then the other letter is the forged one," Dr. Stillman exclaimed, a great wave of joy sweeping across his worn face. "But who could have been interested in doing such a base thing? Surely no one of her companions."

"I don't know; have you the letter? Let me see it."

"Here it is. I don't know why I saved it except to wound myself again and again by re-reading it."

Mr. Jenkins gave a long, sharp whistle. "That is the handwriting of the man I am in search of — the defaulting clerk of Gold, Glitter & Co."

"What do you, an Irish priest, know of Gold, Glitter & Co.?"

In answer, Mr. Jenkins tore off his goggles and threw his priestly broad-

MR. JENKINS REVEALS HIMSELF.

brim on the ground. As Dr. Stillman continued to stare in mild surprise, he drew from an inner pocket of his gown his scrap-book of photographs, and remarked: "Allow me to present these, with the compliments of your humble servant, Abijah Jenkins, of the Detective Bureau, No. —, Great Jones Street, New York. Can be telephoned for, except when on special duty, as at present, from the rooms of the Police Court Tombs Prison."

"Your disguise is perfect; but I do not understand its object."

"It is not necessary that you should. Indeed, I am not sure but you already know too much, since I have made it evident that the rogue I am in search of is a member of Professor Holmes's party. They are clever fellows at disguises. Who can he be? Not the Professor himself. His age is certainly not make up, and the Senhor Silva, whom I at first suspected, was not with them when they came up the river."

"Perhaps he has adopted ladies' attire." The Doctor spoke in fine scorn, but Mr. Jenkins caught at the idea.

"It is perfectly possible. They sometimes do that, you know. There was a Flying Lulu, a clever trapeze performer, who was a great belle, and who turned out to be a man."

"But one of these ladies! You are surely insane."

"No, I am not. That is Bartlett's handwriting, and that is proof positive that Bartlett exists somewhere. I believe he is in the Professor's party, and I propose to find him. I have *carte blanche* as to expense, and the five thousand extra which I shall obtain if I am successful is worth an effort. They have gone up the Madeira, and I shall follow them. Would you like to go with me?"

"Yes, if only to protect them from any annoyance to which you might subject them."

"I shall not annoy them unless I am sure, but I have a shrewd fellow to deal with and I must be shrewd myself. You must promise not to betray me, or I'll not take you with me."

"I promise, and I will even undertake to help you."

"You can do that if you choose. Find out who wrote that letter. It is perfectly natural that you should want to know that for personal reasons. When I know that, I have all the information I want."

"I agree to do this if you will promise, on your side, not to trouble the ladies in any way."

"I shall trouble no one but the author of that letter."

"Then it is a compact."

TAPUYO INDIAN RIVER CRAFT.

When the Doctor and Mr. Jenkins reached San Antonio they found the Bolivian merchant who had assisted the Professor at the Caldeirao ready to ascend the river with his empty barges, having disposed of his cargo of hides and tallow at the rubber depot below. Though of mixed blood, his father having been a mulatto and his mother an Indian, he was intelligent as well as wealthy, for slavery does not exist in Bolivia, and such education as there is, is free to all. The years which had passed over his frosty poll had made him kindly as well as shrewd, and though his face was as twisted as a gnarled apple, the Professor's party had reason to remember long his courtesy to them. He readily agreed to give Brother Dennis and the Doctor passage, and the voyagers ascended the river much more rapidly than the Professor had done. When they reached the "Kettle," he told them of his adventure with the unfortunate tourists, and the Doctor's heart blessed him for his kindness to those dear to him. As their meeting drew near, he grew more and more impatient. The long delays caused by the portages were almost insupportable, and he frequently strode on ahead; at such times acting as pioneer, and striving by every means in his power to hasten their progress.

BOLIVIAN MERCHANT.

They reached the lower rapids of the Bananeiras at nightfall, too late to unload or to attempt to get the boats near the fall that night. But after the evening meal, the Doctor, urged by an impetuosity which he could not himself explain, walked on up the river bank, and, as we have seen, unintentionally alarmed Victoria.

"I would not have frightened you for any consideration," he said, as she slowly regained consciousness, "but I thought I heard my name called, and I naturally hurried forward. I called when I saw that you retreated, but you did not recognize me."

"You have come not a moment too soon," Victoria replied. "I fear the dear Professor is already beyond your power to save."

The Doctor's opinion, after a protracted examination, was not encouraging. He was non-committal to Mrs. Holmes and Delight, but to Victoria he acknowledged that there was very little hope. "We will get him to Exaltacion, where he can have all needed comforts; further than that I cannot promise."

Victoria's anxiety for the Professor was such that she had given the Doctor no opportunity at their first meeting to speak on the subject uppermost in his mind, and until they reached Exaltacion their life on board the barge threw them all so intimately together that there was no chance for private conversation. The Doctor did, indeed, mention his visit at the fazenda of Senhor Polacios and learned with surprise that Victoria had never received the letter which he left for her. He could not mention the forged letter which he had himself received in the presence of the others, and he quietly waited a more convenient opportunity.

Brother Dennis was presented to the party, but, beyond the remark that they had noticed him on the steamer between Santarem and Manaos, he excited no attention.

All breathed a sigh of relief when the barges arrived at the old Jesuit mission bearing the lofty name of the Puerto de Exaltacion de la Santa Cruz. Peace and rest seemed to brood over the decaying town. Silent brown women glided noiselessly about. The plaza with its square of verandahed cottages was like the cloister of some old convent, and the tall crucifixes, and the adobe church, with its curious façade, helped the illusion. Victoria almost fancied that she could see the exiled brothers of the Society of Jesus attending to their priestly avocations. Surely, she thought, if the Professor must die, no more peaceful spot could have been chosen for his last hours than this.

EXALTACION.

The Corregidor, or Prefect of the Department, assigned them apartments in the ancient Collegium. Here, for a time, the Professor's life seemed just to flicker in the socket. Mrs. Holmes and Delight will never forget the Doctor's assiduous kindness during those heart-breaking days; but everyone was kind,—the Corregidor, their faithful servants, Philomena and Graciliano, the stranger priest, Brother Dennis, the Bolivian merchant who had twice helped them on their way, and the friendly Indians of the Pueblo. The sick man realized it all, and there came a day when, freed from fever and pain, he thanked them all sweetly for what they had done. He even looked over Maud's portfolio of drawings which she had made for his proposed book. "The specimens are not all lost," he said with a smile, "for you have figured some of them here." Then he spoke of how he hoped to finish the book when he reached home, and no one had the heart to tell him how faint a possibility there was of this. But the next day and the next passed, and he was no worse. "What a miracle it would be," Victoria said to the Doctor, "if he should recover after all."

"I could have hopes of this," the Doctor replied, "if he could be removed away from the malaria of the river to the higher region of the Serras; there the bracing Andean climate and Nature might effect a cure, but he is not strong enough to bear transportation."

While the Professor lingered in the border-land they were all invited to attend a wedding. It was Philomena who asked them, for she and Graciliano had determined to avail themselves of the opportunities which the mission afforded, and to be Christianly married. Brother Dennis was invited to perform the ceremony, but he somewhat curtly refused. The girls dressed Philomena in white for her bridal, and she looked really handsome in her orange blossoms. "If," groaned Maud, "the bridegroom were not quite such a Caliban!" They attended the ceremonies at the church, and Mrs. Holmes set out a little "refresco" in their best room, while the Professor insisted that the newly-married pair should come to his bedside to receive his congratulations and a considerable gift in money.

In the evening there were Indian dances by some of their new acquaintances in the plaza. There was one which was evidently a religious performance, in which a decorated frame or portable altar, surmounted by crucifixes, was borne by some women, the dancers holding long ribbons attached to it, something after the fashion of braiding the May-pole. This, with its chant in honor of the Virgin, was an inheritance from the early Jesuit Fathers, — a remnant of the passion plays which they taught their converts. Southey, in his "History of Brazil," mentions these autos or plays, which were taught with especial success by Fra Juan Vaz, who, in early life, was one of Charles V.'s musicians, and speaks of the mystery and dramatic dances of the Three Kings of the East, and of St. Michael and the Dragon, with attendant imps, as having been especially popular.

There were other dances which were clearly relics of savagery, — sword dances, and a pretty reel, in which the women, standing in rows, imitated the drawing in of fish lines, and the men acted the part of frolicsome fish. One stately cotillion was of foreign importation and was called — the Corregidor told them — the Lonedone. It was some time before it dawned upon them that this must be a corruption of London. While the dances were progressing Mr. Jenkins took the Doctor aside, and asked him if he had discovered the writer of the forged letter.

"No," replied the young man. "I confess I had forgotten all about it."

"I cannot afford to lose time in this way," the detective replied, somewhat annoyed. "If you do not begin your investigations immediately, I will."

"I will try at once," the Doctor replied; and, approaching Victoria, he asked her if she would like to obtain a bird's-eye view of the plaza from the top of the campanile. She acceded, but, to the Doc-

SWORD DANCE.

tor's chagrin, asked Maud to accompany them. The dancers, as viewed from the summit, made a very pretty spectacle, and fireworks were being displayed at the opposite end of the plaza. Maud suddenly remembered that she had promised to relieve Mrs. Holmes by taking her place at the Professor's bedside, and she hastened down the stairs, saying, "Stay just where you are, and she will know where to find you."

Now was the Doctor's opportunity, and his nervous fingers sought for the letter in an inner pocket.

"How heartless all this gayety seems," Victoria remarked. "How can any one think of marriage when the good Professor is so ill?"

This was not encouraging for the Doctor, for marriage was just the subject uppermost in his mind; but Maud was entering the collegium, and it would not do to lose this chance of speaking to Victoria alone about the letter. He placed it in her hands and asked her if she recognized the handwriting.

"No," she replied wonderingly. "Am I concerned in it? May I read it?"

"Yes, to both questions."

As Victoria read it her wonder deepened. "I do not understand," she said. "Who is this Victoria who writes to you?"

"I thought the letter was from you; it was evidently intended to give me that impression."

"Could you believe that I could be so rude, so unkind? Then, you might well reply that you could not expect anything better of me after the way I demeaned myself at Breves; but I have changed since then, and I have decided that a selfish life is of all lives the most miserable. I want to choose as a career the one in which I can be of the most use in the world."

"Will you let me suggest one way in which you may be a true missionary?"

·

"I think I know what you mean. You are so enthusiastic over your profession that you want to advise me to study medicine. Well, prove that your skill can be of service in the present juncture and I will confess that you have a right to give advice."

"You mean that you will consider any career that I may mark out for you on what conditions?"

"That you cure the Professor."

"I fear that this is beyond human possibility. We can build up where there is anything left to build upon. I know of no remedy in science which can supply the life principle itself."

"But you came to South America to discover new remedies unknown to science. Have you found nothing? Did you see the old witch that the Indian woman told me lived at Obidos and could cure all diseases?"

"I found her. She had only one medicine, a sort of charm. I wrote down the ills it was supposed to cure, and purchased it of her. It promised, however, a great deal too much, and I have no faith in it. I assure you, Miss Delavan, that unless a miracle is wrought he will surely die."

"GO!" VICTORIA EXCLAIMED.

There was a low cry, and Delight, who stumbled across the threshold, fell into Victoria's arms.

"Go," Victoria exclaimed to the startled Doctor, "you have killed her."

"No," Delight replied bravely, "but there is a change; he has fallen into a strange stupor, and mother wants you."

Dr. Stillman hurried away. As he crossed the plaza, Brother

Dennis caught him by the sleeve. "Have you found out," he asked, "who wrote the letter?"

"No," he replied, "but she did not."

"She, which she?"

"Victoria did not write it, bless her, at least if I can cure the Professor; but if I cannot, it is possibly all the same as if she did," and, shaking off his comrade's arm, he entered the sick room.

"Now was there ever such a maniac as that," mused Brother Dennis, "if he can cure the Professor, Victoria did not write that letter; if he cannot she did. The man is a lunatic, a raving lunatic."

CHAPTER XIII.

THE DELECTABLE MOUNTAINS. — CUZCO.

"I CANNOT let him go," Delight moaned, as the two girls crept down the stairs together. "I have felt it all the time and I have battled against it. I would not see; I would not understand. O Victoria, if you knew what my father and I are to each other!"

"I know," Victoria replied, "do you think I have not seen? But you must think of him as well as yourself. Be sure God will do what is best for him." Her own voice sounded strange to Victoria. Delight was her conscience, her standard in matters of religion. And yet, under the need of the moment, here was Victoria guiding her friend to a faith in God, a trust in his infinite loving-kindness, which she hardly knew before that she possessed.

God was leading Delight in a way that she knew not, and in the Valley of the Shadow of Death, through which she was now passing, she was being disciplined to meet the inevitable reality when it should please Him to send it. The two girls stole hand in hand into the sick room.

"His delirium has returned," said Mrs. Holmes. "He keeps talking about the mountains. He probably fancies that he is looking for glaciers in the Andes."

"'These are the Delectable Mountains,'" murmured the Professor, "and they are within sight of His city. You know one of the hills was called 'Clear,' and from it they could see the glory of the place." He talked a little longer, sometimes incoherently, but every now and then they could distinguish the words Delectable Mountains. After a time he roused again, and appeared to be repeating the names of

PERU.

stones. Mrs. Holmes bent her ear to his face. "He is making notes of strata," she said. The Professor shook his head, and whispered more distinctly, "The first was jasper; the second, sapphire; the third, chalcedony; the fourth an emerald."

"He is dying," Delight cried. "It is the heavenly Jerusalem which he sees."

"Pardon me," said the Doctor practically, "he is not dying, — his pulse is normal, his breathing easy. It is only extreme weakness. He has overtaxed his mind to-day with congratulating our good couple, and his brain is weary and a trifle unbalanced, but there is no fever. If we could only start the machinery which is running down, and perhaps we may as well try Justimiama's remedy, since supplying strength is just what it proposed to do." The Doctor opened his medicine chest, and took from it a long snake's skin filled with a dark powder. He passed the skin around the Professor's neck, then crossed it over his heart, and twice around his chest. "There," he said, "let him wear it until morning. The warmth of his body is supposed to waken the powerful agencies of the powdered drugs, and they in their turn will affect the vital organs."

Victoria watched with the sick man that night, but she was very weary, and as he breathed regularly she fell asleep. She was awakened by Delight, who threw her arms about her in the early morning. "Look at my father!" she cried. "Look at him!"

Victoria sprang to her feet, and saw the Professor sitting up in bed, with a bright look illuminating a face that was ruddy with returning health.

"What stimulant have you given me?" he asked. "I feel stronger than I have done since my illness."

The Doctor entered soon after, and appeared as surprised as he was evidently pleased. "I will explain it as far as I can," he said. "Miss Delavan mentioned to me, when we were at Breves together, that she had heard at Para of an old Indian witch doctress named

Justimiama de los Reis, living somewhere near Obidos. When I was there I took the pains to search her out, and to buy some of her remedies from her, the only one seemed to be a certain strength-giving powder administered to patients as a tonic in cases of extreme weakness following protracted illness. I hardly believed in its efficacy myself, for there was much of superstition mingled in Justimiama's account of its preparation, but it seems to have had a revivifying effect upon you, and we will continue its use."

The cloud was lifted. For a little longer the Professor was allowed to work and study and linger with the hearts which clung to him. It frequently happens that a soul is called suddenly, leaving its life work only begun, its friends all unprepared for the parting; but God in his infinite mercy had ordered that the Professor should not be called away until the results of this trip should be fully arranged and left as his legacy to the world. In this brief experience, too, Delight had developed from a shrinking girl to a resolute woman. Something of light-hearted carelessness had gone. The *wholeness* of life, the happy security and confidence that the present state of things must last forever had vanished, but with the dread realization of the certainty of death there had come, too, a higher appreciation of her father's character, a closer knitting of their souls together, and a resolution on Delight's part to be more to him while he lived, and to fit herself to continue his work, — to make her young life carry on his valuable one after he had gone.

The morning brought the Doctor a triple pleasure. The Professor was certainly much stronger; he was dressed and sat up for an hour; and the recovery of the Professor meant not only the saving of the life of one good man, but the discovery of a remedy new to science, and the reward promised the Doctor in the Campanile on the eve of Philomena's wedding.

Justimiama's powder was indeed wonder-working. In three days the Professor was able to take his seat in the saddle, and in three more the party started for the Andes. It was fictitious strength, no doubt, but the stimulus lasted until the cool mountain breezes supplemented it with a natural tonic, and brought back vigor to the nerves and muscles, and a healthy glow to the faded cheek.

Philomena and Graciliano accompanied them, and Mr. Jenkins also made one of the party. Before leaving Exaltacion he confided to the Doctor that under different pretexts he had examined the chirography of every member of the party, without being able to discover anything like the Spencerian flourish of Mr. Bartlett's hand. "I have lost my man," he said despairingly. "Somewhere on the route he has left them. I acknowledge myself baffled, and shall now return to New York. I have already nearly traversed the continent, and my shortest course now is to cross the Andes with you, and, leaving you somewhere in the neighborhood of Lake Titicaca, embark at Arequipa for Panama."

The Doctor sighed, "And I must do the same," he said. "The Professor intends to follow up the Andean chains into Ecuador, but my allowance for travelling expenses is already overdrawn, and, much as I would like to accompany him, I shall be obliged to take the quicker route for home. By the way," he remarked suddenly, "now that you acknowledge your absurd suspicions unfounded, I insist on your abandoning your disguise and appearing in your true character."

"They have all penetrated it," Mr. Jenkins replied sheepishly. "Miss Victoria was the first to suspect me. She's a sharp, quick one, she is. 'Mr. Jenkins,' she said, 'I do not understand why you should feel it necessary to disguise yourself from us, but since you think best to do so, I will keep your secret.' 'Thank you, Ma'am,' I replied, 'you are very kind;' and then I was fool enough to ask Miss Maud to let me look at the Professor's note-books, pretending that I wished to compare his discoveries with some made by the early Jesuits, — Padre Cristoval, or Padre goodness knows who. I had a scrap from one of Gold & Glitter's account-books, which I placed beside the Professor's hieroglyphics. They were no more alike than an operatic score is to a cuneiform inscription. But her sharp eyes saw what I was about, and she read off as glibly as you please, 'Gold & Glitter, in account with Baring Brothers,' etc. 'Mr. Jenkins,' says she, 'do you mean to imply that you suspect that heavenly man, the Professor?' 'Oh no, Miss,' I replied, 'but here is a bit of Mr. Bartlett's handwriting, and it resembles very much a communication addressed to Dr. Stillman, which must have come from some one in your company, so you may judge for yourself what cause I have for my investigations.' 'There is no one with us who writes like that,' she said, examining the characters very carefully. 'If you will give me this scrap of paper I will do my best to ascertain the writer of the letter of which you speak. I have my own reasons for wishing to know.' 'Certainly, Miss,' I replied, 'and meantime,'—'Meantime, I will keep your secret.' The next to find me out was Mrs. Holmes. She suspected me when I would not marry the Indian couple. Miss Delight was the most unsuspicious of all, but the night that we all thought her father would not live she caught me by the arm and asked me to come in and read the prayers for the dying. 'I can't,' said I. 'I'm not such a hypocrite as that.' 'I know you are not of the same communion,' she went on, 'but there is no clergyman here, and you are both Christians. Surely you cannot refuse to speak to him of Jesus and support him through this terrible hour. Your religion does not forbid you to pray for him, does it?' 'No, indeed,' said I, 'and I do pray for him with all my heart.' 'Then, come with me,' she pleaded, and I, I couldn't stand it another minute. 'Miss Delight,' said I, 'don't you know me?' She gave me a wild look. 'O, Mr. Jenkins,' she cried, 'now I know why you have been so kind; we have another friend with us.' She didn't resent my coming like the other girls, and I felt a thousand times meaner than I have ever felt in the entire course of my profession."

Mr. Jenkins, after this, appeared as the photographer, carrying his sneak-box before him on the pommel of his saddle. His beard had begun to grow, giving him a bristling and savage look, but his heart

GATES HEWN IN THE ROCK.

had been won by Delight's kindness, and he constituted himself her especial cavalier.

It would take too long to tell of their journey, through gates hewn in the rock as by supernatural power, to the wonderful Andean ranges. They floated on lonely streams, brushed only by white cranes and the Indian's paddle; they camped under groves of tamarind trees, and joined a mule train across the desolate pampas, reaching at last the noble Serras, snow-crowned and silver-hearted. They visited more than one silver mine between Santa Cruz and Cochabamba, and Victoria purchased several pieces of table service, chafing dishes, and graceful pitchers decorated by native workmen. Their longest pause was made at La Paz, the commercial metropolis of Bolivia, whose tile-roofed houses nestle at the foot of the snow-crowned Illimani. Here they found European residents and French fashions, a theatre, a museum, and much of the activity of business. The alameda or public park was the fashionable resort *before breakfast*, the ladies of the city appearing on the promenade at that time in ball costumes, with white kid gloves and satin slippers. The Bolivian ladies were graceful and fearless horsewomen. Slender, pale and sweet, they reminded Maud of the tube-roses which grew so plentifully in their gardens, and whose carven blossoms almost invariably decorated their jetty braids, tucked coquettishly just behind the ear.

Over the dry table-lands they now rode to the heart of the Andes, the grand procession stretching to the north and south, peak after peak shouldering each other away in magnificent perspective. They saw the peaks burning with sunset or touched with the tender beauty of dawn, they watched the condor fluttering over horrible precipices, and trains of llamas threading dizzy passes. They sailed across dreary Lake Titicaca, once the site of the pleasure palaces of the Incas, now a waste of tombs, and rested a few days at the little town of Puno on their way to the royal city of Cuzco.

The way was long, but to the Doctor it seemed cruelly short, for at Cuzco it was now decided that Mr. Jenkins and he were to separate from the others. The entire journey was a triumphal march to the Professor, his cure was complete, and with every step he grew stronger and apparently more youthful, but the Doctor saw with

PEAK AFTER PEAK.

some disappointment that Victoria had taken for granted that the career which he wished to propose to her was that of a student of medicine.

"At Cuzco," he said to himself, "I must 'put it to the test and win or lose it all.'" But Victoria made the task of approaching the subject a very difficult one. Whenever he spoke of the future she turned the conversations so easily from a sentimental to a scientific tone.

"I mean to pursue my professional studies in Switzerland," she said. "Let me see; where is that medical school for women? Zurich or Geneva? I really think you ought to be satisfied, Dr. Stillman. You have succeeded in bringing me over to your theories of life, its seriousness and responsibility."

"That is a great deal, I confess," he replied.

"And you have made at least one startling discovery in medicine which is going to be famous. Now confess that your trip to the South has been widely successful."

"More so than I could have dreamed."

"And you are a perfectly satisfied man?"

"I would be if"—

"Oh, '*if*'— So would everybody if— For my part, I think you are very unreasonable. Now I am satisfied, perfectly. I am going straight back to Vassar to finish my education. I shall study all the harder, now that I have a special object in view. There are so many things to learn, and so little time in which to learn them, even if one aspires to be only generally educated. I think our college course is entirely too short. What can one learn of history, for instance, in four years? How long did Prescott study before he wrote his 'Conquest of Peru'?"

"And yet it has not taken us long to read the result of his study."

"How we ought to honor such men for making the obscure passages of our history so easily attainable. What would this imperial city of the Incas mean to us without the introduction which that fascinating book gives to us? And to think that we are to see the ruins of the palaces and temples of the Incas. It is certainly the most wonderful city in the new world."

"It has been called the Rome of South America."

"It seems to me more like Egypt. The cyclopean walls of dark stone — granite or porphyry, the Professor says, blackened by time, seem to me as solemn and as venerable as the Pyramids."

INCA HUAYNA OCAPAL.

"There is something Egyptian, too, in the cast of features of the Inca dynasty."

"Yes, they were the Pharaohs of Peru."

"And Pizarro was Moses?"

"No, indeed, I think the invasion of the Spaniards a long story of cruelty and treachery. Why could n't Charles V. have been contented with his Sevillian gardens, and have left the native monarchs in possession of their pleasure grounds and terraces in the valley of the Yucay."

"And yet is there not a spirit of romance in the story of Pizarro's adventures? He sailed, you know, with only a handful of companions from Panama, — a forlorn hope to explore the coast of Peru. He found a wealthy and powerful nation, and, returning to Spain, obtained a patent from Charles V. to conquer the country, which was effected with only an insignificant company of adventurers."

"You forget that he took advantage of dissensions between the royal brothers, and incited one political party against another, obtaining his desires at last by perfidy instead of by lawful conquest. I could forgive Pizarro but for his treachery to poor Atahualpa."

INCA TUPAC YUPANGRU.

Their stay at Cuzco was one of great interest. They visited the church at St. Domingo, built on the ruins of the Temple of the Sun, and made excursions to fortresses "on dizzy crags and forbidding passes." The more that they saw of the ancient remains, whether of architecture, sculpture, or pottery, the more they wondered at the height to which civilization had arrived in a race surrounded on all sides by untutored savages. "I wish we could have seen some of the golden and silver vases which adorned the temples and palaces," Maud said. "I can't forgive Pizarro for melting them up so ruthlessly. Only think! the gold distributed as booty to the Spanish soldiers on the taking of Cuzco amounted in value to fifteen millions of dollars, and much of this was curiously wrought in jewelry and objects of art."

INCA YUPAKKUI.

"What seems strange to me," said Delight, "is that they could have done so much without iron."

"Silver must have taken its place. You know Pizarro caused his horses to be shod with silver, for lack of the stronger metal."

EFFIGY.

"The Peruvians had no horses, and when the natives first saw the Spanish cavaliers they imagined that horse and rider were one animal,—terrible centaurs, with power to command the lightning and the thunder with clumsy blunderbusses."

"These ruins have such a Titanic and ancient look," said Victoria, "that I can scarcely realize that the taking of Cuzco by Pizarro occurred as late as 1533, and that the last descendant of the Incas was cruelly executed in our own century."

The Professor was of the opinion that many of the immense ruins not only out-dated the Spanish conquest, but were contemporaneous with some of the remains in Egypt and Persia.

They found much to entertain them in modern Cuzco, its churches and convents, as well as in the souvenirs of the past. There was the Cathedral with its two bell-towers, and the pretty legend in regard to the missing bell. Two bells of the same size had been cast for these towers and christened respectively Maria and Magdalena. But the ship bearing the Magdalena foundered at sea, and now, when the Maria tolls or sends forth a joyous peal, the fishermen say that they can hear her sister chiming an answer, though buried deep beneath the sea.

SPANISH MONASTERY.

They saw the great effigies which, on the festival of the *Señor de los Temblores* (Christ of the Earthquakes), parade the city. They were not unlike the images used for the same purpose in Passion week in Seville.

Maud made a note of the imbecile creatures. San Blas, from whom a quarter in the city is named, was dressed like a Spanish courtier of the time of Charles V., with an angel attendant perched upon a spiral spring, shading his saintship with a pink silk parasol. Nearly all of the figures were arranged with these springs, which gives them a swaying, bobbing motion as their litters are carried through the streets. San Benito follows next in the procession, — a negro saint resembling Brudder Bones; and next comes Saint Christopher, leaning on a palm-tree staff, and costumed like an Assyrian king. Then follows St. Joseph, the carpenter, dressed like a Carmelite monk, and carrying a saw as a symbol of his craft.

EFFIGY.

Next appears the effigy of the Blessed Virgin, a wax doll in the toilette of an empress, loaded with jewels, her blond hair curled and powdered, and a fan in her dainty hand. Her dress is embroidered with pearls, a collar of rubies supports her immense lace ruff, and her diadem is of immense value. Her glass eyes are contrived by clock-work to revolve rapidly, and so she progresses, curtesying, ogling, while the crowd shriek their admiration. The most horrible image of all is the Christ, stretched upon a cross, blackened by age, having never been retouched since the Emperor Charles sent it from Cadiz, as hideous as an idol, and draped with a tawdry petticoat of lace, looped by a ribbon.

"Tell me," said Maud, "was the ancient Sun worship of the Peruvians worse than this idolatry?"

"It is possible," replied the Professor, "that when we consider all

EFFIGY.

its degrading features we must confess that it was. The religious legends, though many of them poetical, were manifestly invented to give divine authority to the reign of the Incas. According to tradition the time was when the ancient races were plunged in barbarism. The Sun, taking compassion on their degraded condition, sent two of his children, Manco Capac and Mama Oella Huaco to gather the natives into communities and teach them the arts of civilized life. They bore with them a golden wedge, and were directed to take up their residence on the spot where the sacred emblem should without effort sink into the ground. At Cuzco the wedge sank into the earth and disappeared forever. Here the children of the Sun established their residence, and entered upon their beneficent mission, and became the ancestors of the Incas."

So the days slipped by and the time came when the Professor was anxious to continue his journey to Lima and the north, and Mr. Jenkins was impatient to embark. Circumstances favored the Doctor and, just before he left, gave him the opportunity which he sought. The environs of Cuzco furnish much that is interesting, and they had

THE FAREWELL TREE.

made a number of excursions from their lodgings in the queer little house in the Calle de las Heladeiras, or street of sherbets and ices. One of the most enjoyable of these was to the Fortress of Sacsahuaman, whose Titanic terraces might have served as the foundations for the Tower of Babel. Their last excursion was to the Convent of Recolletta, and to a gorge in the mountains called the Ladder to Heaven. They had picnicked in the valley; Maud was sketching; the Professor and Mrs. Holmes resting, — when their guide told them of a famous old tree a little further on toward San Sebastian, called the "Tree of Farewells." "When any one leaves Cuzco, his relations and friends accompany him as far as this tree," said the man, "and then bid him God speed, and all who there part in friendship are sure to meet again. It is a very ancient tree. It was planted by the Inca Capac Yupanqui."

"I would like to take a photograph of it," said Mr. Jenkins.

"Let us ride over and bid the Doctor and Mr. Jenkins *bon voyage* under its shadow," Delight suggested.

"You and Victoria can go," said Mrs. Holmes, "we will await you here."

Arrived under the tree Mr. Jenkins posed Victoria and the Doctor in the act of bidding each other farewell, while he retired to a little distance to bring them into focus. Then Victoria and the Doctor photographed Delight and Mr. Jenkins, and, having each plucked a leaf of the magical tree as a souvenir, they turned the noses of their mules toward the convent. What possessed the fleet little animal upon which Delight rode? It scrambled over the ground in a perfect fury of impatience, followed by Mr. Jenkins, who, lashing his own beast as best he might, could only approach within a few yards, while Victoria and the Doctor were left far behind. It was then that the Doctor saw and seized his opportunity.

"Victoria," he said, "you know that the charm goes for nothing unless we really wish to meet again."

"I'm sure I wish it, don't you?" she replied.

"That depends upon the answer you make to this question. You have done me great honor already; will you make me still happier by consenting some day to be my wife?"

Victoria reined in her mule and looked at the Doctor with unfeigned astonishment. "Why, you are just like the rest," she said.

"And are you going to give me the same answer which you have given 'the rest'? Tell me at least that you will think it over."

"That is precisely what I have always told the others, and the more I thought about it the less I liked the idea."

"Then, Victoria, accept me without thinking about it."

"I can't under the circumstances. You know 'It is well to be off with the old love, before one is on with the new.'"

"Then I am to understand that you are already engaged?"

"No! I'm only 'thinking it over,' and, as I told you, I don't like it. But I could n't think of your case at the same time; it would n't be honest and true.'"

"You might set down my name as a possible candidate for the situation when next it falls vacant."

"Don't speak with such infinite scorn. I am not to blame, am I, if people ask me to consider such things."

"You might at least decline to encourage them."

"So I do. I decline to encourage you, but it does not seem to please you. Come, Dr. Stillman, you have asked me in what way Vassar girls are different from others differently educated. This is one of their peculiarities, — they are more cautious in taking a step of this kind. We are more sufficient to ourselves, less dependent upon marriage in every way, and more *exigeante*."

"I see you do not care for me, or you could not be so coolly calculating."

"I beg your pardon, Dr. Stillman, I do care for you; so much so that I am not willing you should betroth yourself to a half-hearted girl. You have been very good to me, and I cannot trifle with you. You have my unqualified respect and esteem. You have wakened my sense of accountability, my mental and moral energies, but you have not wakened my heart, — perhaps I have none. Your work has been successful. When you consider the material you ought to be content. No, you only imagine that you love me," she added, as she noticed the look of keen anguish in the young man's face. "I have heard that young physicians are apt to feel a deep interest in their first patients, which is never experienced for later ones. I have been your first patient. You have cured me of lassitude and indifference to the real objects of life. I've no doubt you will do the same for others without fancying yourself in love with them. You are my true friend, and I give you my hand again, as I did under the parting tree, wishing you for all your life a hearty *bon voyage*."

According to the correct thing in romances the Doctor should have pressed Victoria's hand to his lips at this juncture, but he could not get his refractory mule near enough even to take it, and he contented himself with doing it in imagination.

The next morning he departed with Mr. Jenkins for Arequipa, and the Professor and his charge took the broad road of the Incas for the north. It was noticed by her companions that Victoria was absent-minded and silent. In reality she was submitting herself to severe self-criticism. "I have not treated him like the rest," she said to herself, "which proves that I do not feel toward him as I do to the rest. I have always been reasonable, and told them that I would consider the matter, ascertaining in due time that I did not care for them a particle. I have been unreasonable with Dr. Stillman and dismissed him without the least consideration. Does that prove that I perversely do care for him a little? If it does, all I have to say is that it is quite too late."

CHAPTER XIV.

IN THE HEART OF A VOLCANO.

THE road on which they were now travelling was cut out of the mountains from ten to eleven thousand feet above the level of the sea, three thousand feet higher than the Hospice of St. Bernard, and yet for some distance from Cuzco, instead of an Alpine region of perpetual snow, they journeyed through fertile valleys and luxuriant forests. Notable among the new vegetation were the Rhexia, or king of shrubs. Its immense violet flowers were not more curious than its variegated stem and its leaves, green above and lined with orange. They passed through cinchona forests, from whose bark the great staple remedy, quinine, is manufactured.

"Do you suppose the Incas used it?" Maud asked.

"Possibly," the Professor replied, "but its good qualities were only announced to the world in 1638 by the Countess of Cinchon, the wife of the Spanish viceroy."

Their road led them at times by the side of roaring cataracts. The Apurimac, the principal of the Peruvian rivers, is flanked for a part of its course with fluted shafts, and walls of basaltic formation, forming tall cliffs and cañons through which the yellow waters foam and swirl. Nothing could have been more beautiful than this enchanted region; but with Victoria's distrust of the wisdom of her decision there sprang up in her a demon of doubt which poisoned for a time her friendship for Maud. It was caused by the forged letter which the Doctor had left in her possession. Who could have written it was a question which she had asked herself again and again without obtaining any light. Someone had done so who had first read the

Doctor's letter to her, and who wished to make mischief between them. She could not attribute such an action to either of her old friends, Delight or her mother, but Maud was more of a stranger. Maud had always expressed open admiration for the Doctor; was it not possible that she had done this thing through envy and jealousy? So, while her heart was troubled with the greater discontent, this little canker-worm of suspicion fed and fattened, and poisoned all the delightful present.

At Cuzco they had been joined by an agreeable travelling companion, a Mr. Hartley from the United States, who had come to South America as a newspaper correspondent to report the war between Chili and Peru, but who had remained out of love for the country and a slight interest in some silver mines. He had made himself an encyclopædia of information, and long and interesting were his disquisitions on guano and politics, topics which Victoria declared were equally disagreeable. He had examined the Chilian fleet and pronounced the country able to blockade the Pacific ports of the United States at any time. The Professor and he had many an argument over the reduction of the United States, the Professor asserting that the glory of our country was in her weakness as a military power, and that war was a relic of barbarism. The rest of the party found Mr. Hartley extremely amusing, for he was a keen observer and a racy story-teller. He had made many acquaintances during his stay in the country, and he asked their permission to introduce them to a certain Señor and Señora Chrysostomo Nepomuceno Palacido Joaquim do Santo Thyrso y Mirandella who resided at Quito. "I shall certainly die of an indigestion of these long names," Victoria had asserted; but Maud, who enjoyed foreigners, was sure that it would be pleasant to make the acquaintance of some Spanish Americans as well as of the Brazilians, who, being of Portuguese extraction, preserved certain race differences as well as peculiarities arising from different surroundings.

They followed the great Inca road, the same over which Pizarro marched to the conquest of Cuzco, as far as the town of Oroya, travelling by mule-train. Here for the first time in their South American journey they were able to enjoy the conveniences of transportation by railroad, and a North American railroad at that. From Callao through Lima, across the western range of the Andes, a railroad has been built by the enterprise of Mr. Meigs, an engineer from the United States. It has been well described in Scribner's Magazine by Mr. J. Eglinton Montgomery as a railroad in the clouds. Over this wonderful line the party now passed, playing hide and seek with the roaring, rushing Rimac, down whose valley the road ran, crossing the river again and again, doubling, winding to avoid steep grades, gliding along dizzy trestle work which showed like spiders' webs across the gorges, plunging into tunnels, crossing viaducts, dashing down terrible inclines in their swift descent from the eternal snows to the sea level.

At the very summit of the Andes they entered the Tuñel de la Cima, only 136 feet lower than Mont Blanc, and 3,847 feet long. Snowy peaks were all around them; the region was one of Alpine grandeur and desolation. After leaving the tunnel they zigzagged down the valley, watching the peasants stumbling down the ladder-like passes, driving their llamas to market laden with produce, and trudging beside them on foot rather than pay the fare on the railroad. Cactus now sprang up on the sunny slopes in pillar-like stalks adorned with scarlet tassels. Further down they passed across " Los Infiernillos," or Little Hells, where the river threaded a chasm walled by perpendicular masses of porphyry, 1,000 to 1,500 feet high.

They looked out upon straw-thatched adobe huts, where dwelt the "Children of the Mist," and at one point in their descent passed through so many successive peaks that they threaded twenty-two tunnels in a distance of only fifteen miles. Maud's eyes glowed with

THE APURIMAC.

excitement for she had accepted a ride in the engine which the others had refused. She declined Mr. Hartley's support, but folded her arms tightly as the train seemed to plunge straight down to destruction. When they slackened speed and conversation was possible, she turned to her companion with the exclamation, "It is like being hurled from the cannon's mouth! I never experienced so glorious a sensation."

They remained only three days at Lima, for the Professor did not care for sight-seeing, and the volcanoes clustering around Quito away in the North, drew his heart like a magnet. Their drives around the Ciudad de los Reyes, or City of the Kings, showed them adobe houses built around

ANDEAN PEAKS.

regular squares and with some pretence to architecture. The Cathedral, especially, was suggestively Moorish, and the long colonnades skirting three sides of the nine-acre Plaza Mayor were cool and shady. They visited Pizarro's palace and the University of San Marco, with its wonderful wood carving, on the Plaza de la Inquisicion.

Their next stop was at Callao, celebrated for its earthquakes and its fortress, and from this point took passage on a steamer of the Pacific Mail Line for Guayaquil. It was during this short voyage that Maud felt Victoria's coldness and perceived that something was wrong. She attempted to be gracious and chatty, but Victoria repulsed her advances; and Maud, hurt and a little indignant at this unjust and seemingly capricious behavior, retired within herself, and, devoting herself to her sketching, allowed her attention to be occupied by Mr. Hartley's vivacious description of his friends at Quito.

"They are the gentlest, most simple-minded people in the world," he said, "and yet they are as ceremonious in their manners as the courtiers of old Spain. They make the utmost possible of their long names, repeating them and reiterating them, and dwelling with great complacency on the compounds and the annexes. You know or perhaps you don't know, that near relatives may have slight variations of the family name, owing to their absurd habit of perpetuating the maiden name of the mother, linked by a 'y' to that of the father."

"Oh! yes," Maud replied, "we know all about that. It gave us a great deal of bother in Brazil."

"Here is an invitation to dinner from my friend," continued Mr. Hartley. "He does not begin as we would, 'Mr. and Mrs. Mirandella request the pleasure,' etc., but flourishes off in this style, —

"'Señor Chrysostomo Nepomuceno Palacido Joaquim do Santo Thyrso y Mirandella presents the compliments of his mother, the Señora Anastasia Zoe

PIZARRO ON THE ROAD TO CUZCO

Melendes do Santo Thyrso y Mirandella, and of his wife the Señora Candida Maria Encarnacão Souza y Silva do Santo Thyrso y Mirandella, and begs the felicity' —"

Maud's keen eye ran over the invitation. "The Spaniards spell Señor and Señora without the h which the Portuguese insert," she remarked. "But Souza y Silva is a Portuguese name. Why, it is the very same! Can it be possible that this is my little Candida of the Convent of Bom Successo in Lisbon?"

"I believe Doña Mirandella is of Portuguese extraction," Mr. Hartley replied, "she has been married only a year or so; it might be possible."

The others, attracted by Maud's exclamation, joined in the discussion, but they all thought it quite unlikely that Senhor Silva's sister could be here while he thought her still unmarried and in Lisbon.

"It does seem strange," Maud admitted, while all the doubts which she had ever harbored in regard to the man swarmed back upon her.

"Quito was one of the points where we were to hear from the Senhor," said Mrs. Holmes. "We have missed his letters so far, perhaps we are now to be more fortunate."

Mrs. Holmes was a firm believer in the Senhor. She would not credit Graciliano's assertion that the servants were told to leave them at the most disheartening point of their journey, but preferred to attribute this conduct to their own treachery.

At Guayaquil they were transferred to a smaller steamer which carried them a short distance up the river Guayas on their way to Quito. Taking once more to mountain travel at the little town of Bodegas, they found themselves among the volcanoes. Snowy ranges were all around them, but as they rode into the town of Rio Bamba one great peak dominated the landscape, — a majestic cone, pure white, and of a grandeur and symmetry which awakened universal cries of admiration.

"What mountain is that?" Victoria asked of their guide, and she never forgot the withering scorn with which the man repeated the name Chimborazo. It was as though a stranger had stood before Niagara and had turned to an American with the question, "What do you call that cascade?"

The Professor was in his glory. He recognized every peak at sight, and repeated the names of each of the fifty-one Andean volcanoes.

CHIMBORAZO.

"Of all this number," he said, "twenty are in the neighborhood of Quito. Three of these are active, five dormant, and the rest extinct. Chimborazo is the monarch of them all. Caraguairiazo is called the wife of Chimborazo."

"Chimborazo is the highest mountain in the world, is it not?" asked Delight.

"No, my dear," the Professor replied, "it was long considered so, but Aconcagua of Chili overtops it. Cotopaxi is off to the east there, smoking its calumet like a sleepy Indian wrapped in his blanket. He grumbles at times in his dreams, showing that if he should wake and take to the war-path he would be dangerous. Altar, farther to the south, has eight cones, and Sangai, its companion, has been a spit-fire for three centuries. It is probable that all of these volcanoes are but chimneys for one single furnace.

"Think what a horrible fiery gulf this beautiful region roofs. It is enough to chill the blood with terror."

"It does not chill me in the least," replied Victoria. "On the contrary it rather warms my imagination. Did you ever read 'Bulwer's Coming Race.' He believes the new Utopia to be underground, and that the beings who inhabit the mysterious recesses and subterranean caverns are endowed with a magical force called vril, surpassing electricity in its effects. They fly at will, and do

COTOPAXI.

many astonishing things, and the women are all stronger and wiser than the men. It is a very ingenious book. One half believes while reading it."

"Father," exclaimed Delight, "can we descend a volcano? I would enjoy it above all things."

"I hope to, my child," replied the Professor. "We will see what can be done when we reach Quito."

"My friends will be able to tell you what craters are practicable," said Mr. Hartley, "and will render you every assistance in their power."

The morning after their arrival in Quito, Mr. Hartley fulfilled his promise by bringing Señor Mirandella to call upon them. He informed them that his family were at his *hacienda* or country seat, in the mountains, to which he invited them most warmly, offering to ride out with them and assuring them of a hearty welcome. Maud made a few inquiries, and being convinced that Señora Mirandella was no other than her little Lisbonese friend, was anxious to see her; and the Professor, when informed that the hacienda was only one day's journey from the volcano of Pichincha and that its crater was frequently visited by tourists, at once accepted the hospitable invitation of their new acquaintance. Señor Mirandella sent a courier ahead to inform his wife of their coming, and the excursion was set for the following day. The afternoon they devoted to Quito, which, unlike the regular city of Lima with its squares and boulevards, they found a most picturesque huddle of houses clambering the sides of the hills on which it is built and straggling along the sides of the two ravines which intersected it. All around them rose the mountains, eight great peaks being visible from the city. The houses were usually of but one story, on account of the frequency of earthquakes, the last having nearly wrecked the place. Rich fruits and flowers were noticeable everywhere, and fountains gushed in abundance, but they were told that the water

SPANISH AMERICA.

impregnated with various minerals was productive of elephantiasis, though in other respects the mountain city was one of the most healthful in South America.

Victoria bought pieces of the gold lace made by the women, and all greatly enjoyed their visits to the libraries.

The next morning a gay cavalcade started up the slopes of the volcano of Pichincha. They rode through a most beautiful and fertile region, and Delight frequently exclaimed with pleasure as a new fern was handed her. Señor Mirandella assured her that the region boasted one hundred and forty species. The bamboo, king of grasses, grew rankly by the roadside, and fuchsias were everywhere abundant.

They reached the hacienda at noon and were warmly welcomed by the ladies, the wife of Señor Mirandella proving to be indeed Maud's friend. She had studied English at the convent in Lisbon, and she greeted them with an enthusiastic " I am delightful to see you!"

She ushered them at once to a cool dining-room and served them to *chirimoyas*, — a fruit which Mr. Hartley declared to be spiritualized strawberries, — and to some delicious ices and cakes. They spent the afternoon in the lovely garden, where they found exquisite flowers of nearly every kind except roses, for the queen of the garden does not flourish in South America.

"The mimosæ are my favorites," said their hostess, "for, see, they fold their little hands and say their prayers every evening before they sleep."

The girls spoke of their odd meeting with her brother, Señor Silva, and she looked up in a startled way.

"Is Jesuino in Brazil?" she asked. " I did not know it."

"Not Jesuino," Maud replied, "but your half-brother, the Señor Palacios y Silva."

"But I have no half brother," Señora Mirandella replied wonderingly.

"Are you sure of this?" Maud asked, and then she reviewed the entire story of their meeting with the Senhor on ship-board; but the more she explained the more mysterious it all became.

The gentlemen were called in to give their opinion, and Mr. Hartley was certain that the Senhor was a clever sharper who had claimed relationship with Maud's friends, because he saw that it would give him a passport to their society.

"But how did he know all about the Silvas?" Maud asked.

"Maud, dear," Delight exclaimed, "I remember distinctly now. When he said his name was Silva you told him all about your Lisbonese friends, and he merely listened until you had ended and then asserted his relationship."

"And have you no friends by the name of Palacios?" Maud asked.

"None whatever," the Señora replied.

"Then I am afraid," said Mr. Hartley, "that it is a clear case against the Senhor."

"I don't like to believe this," said the Professor. "He was a very interesting man."

"There were many suspicious circumstances," said Delight, "you know what Mr. Jenkins thought."

"Dear me," groaned Maud, "if it had not been for my assurance that I knew his family he might have been arrested by this time."

"What do you mean?" Victoria asked proudly. "Mr. Jenkins was always suspecting some one; but, however bad the Senhor may be, I do not see that we have any proof that he was Gold & Glitter's defaulting cashier."

"No real proof," Maud assented, "and yet I am morally certain that he is the man."

Señor Mirandella now called for music, and his wife was induced to sing Tennyson's "Brook," and again Maud listened to the familiar words with the odd accent which had so amused her in Lisbon, —

"I charter, charter, as I go to join the breeming reever."

Then the Professor talked volcanoes, and Victoria listened without hearing,—it seemed to her that she had been treading on volcanic ground. She was convinced that the Senhor was an evil man, and she shuddered as she thought how nearly she had come to placing the greatest trust of life in him.

The next morning they set out for the summit of Pichincha, which they reached before noon, and began the hazardous descent of the crater. They were fastened to each other by a long line, and descended on foot in Indian file, stepping cautiously over deep crevices, and keeping close to the precipitous side of the mountain. They found gentians and violets growing close to sulphur-coated stones. The basin was 2,500 feet deep and 1,500 feet in diameter. In its centre there was a pile of stones,—the cone or chimney of eruption, two hundred and sixty feet high.

"What a Valley of the Shadow of Death it is!" Maud exclaimed, as they reached the bottom, after two hours and a half of tedious climbing, and the party rested, fanning themselves with their hats.

"It would be a good place in which to read 'Dante's Inferno,'" Delight suggested.

"Or to sing the 'De Profundis,'" Victoria added.

After resting, the party dispersed,—some picking up specimens of lava and minerals, others assisting in the preparation of lunch, which was partaken of in the shadow of the cone. It seemed to them all that their merriment was a little strained, and that their voices sounded hollow in this great caldron.

"It is like Sodom and Gomorrah," Victoria exclaimed. "What if the fiery gulf should open under our feet now. I certainly feel an uncomfortable premonition of evil, and I wish we had not come. We seem to be daring the unseen powers to do their worst by bringing our sport into the very throat of the monster."

The Professor endeavored to prove that the volcano was extinct, and while searching through his memorandum book for the date of its last eruption he was suddenly startled by the discovery of a letter addressed to Victoria.

"Dear me," he ejaculated, "how forgetful I am. I found this letter waiting for us at Quito, but have been so busy with other matters that it never occurred to me to hand it to you."

GRACILIANO AND THE LETTER.

The manner of its presentation was so abrupt that all eyes were fixed upon Victoria, who was strangely affected by its receipt. She did not open it for several moments, but stared fixedly at the address, at first vaguely striving to realize why it seemed so familiar, and then, suddenly realizing that this was the hand which had written the forged letter to the Doctor, she tore it open, and, without glancing at the contents, read only the signature, José Ignacio da Silva y Palacios.

A great wave of crimson swept across her face and throat. He had done this; then she could believe anything of him. "Maud," she said, extending her hand frankly, "I have done you a great wrong. Will you forgive me?"

"Why certainly; what was it?" Maud replied in a breath.

"I would rather not tell you, for you would be perfectly justified in being deeply offended that I could have imagined you capable of the mean action whose author I have just discovered. Graciliano, if you will fasten this letter to one of your arrows and shoot it so exactly that it will fall just within the cone-chimney of the volcano, I will be greatly obliged to you."

Graciliano stepped up grinning, but Maud stopped him. "One instant, Victoria," she pleaded. "Will you not let me compare the address on that envelope with some writing which Mr. Jenkins left with me. It will either prove or disprove the suspicion which I expressed last evening, for this paper which I hold in my hand was written by that Mr. Bartlett."

"And my letter," Victoria replied, "is from Senhor Palacios, and is the very hand in which a letter purporting to be from me was written to Dr. Stillman. He has proved himself a forger in one matter; it would be perfectly consistent if he were shown to be a scoundrel through and through."

Victoria reopened the letter which she had crumpled in her indignation and glanced it over. She could not show Maud the first page, for in it the Senhor had taken an unmanly advantage of their undecided relations to each other, and had assumed a binding engagement. This enraged Victoria still further, and she ran over the pages with kindling eye. Luckily the last sheet contained nothing which all might not read, and was indeed intended to be passed from hand to hand and read by the entire party.

"Take it!" Victoria exclaimed, "and I trust it may realize your worst suspicions."

The two sheets of paper were compared in silence, for the chirography was identical.

"A volcano has indeed opened under our feet," said the Professor.

"A pretty active one too," grumbled Maud, "and once more where, oh, where is Mr. Jenkins? and why didn't I show him that sketch which I made of the Senhor with blond hair?"

"Only because you were too just to throw suspicion upon him while you still thought that he was the brother of your friend here, and consequently innocent," Delight replied.

"You have enough evidence now to convict and send him to Sing Sing," Mr. Hartley remarked.

"Provided that he can be caught," Maud replied dryly.

"You had better not inform our officials," Señor Mirandella advised. "They are so inefficient that he would slip through their fingers."

"And yet," added his pretty wife, "I would like to have him apprehended if only for pretending himself to be my bruzzer."

"I can send everything by mail straight to Gold & Glitter," Maud suggested.

"We will reach New York as soon as a letter," the Professor objected, "and can give clearer testimony than could be written."

"You had better telegraph from the first station," Mr. Hartley advised, "and state that proofs, etc., are on the way." And this plan was afterwards followed.

"Now," said Victoria, after the tumult of discussion had a little subsided. "If any of you *can* sing 'De Profundis' I wish you would, for I certainly feel that we have been taken out of the depths, in escaping from that man's society."

"We need the Doctor to sing anything," Delight replied, and Mrs. Holmes echoed a regret for his absence.

Rested and refreshed, the party began the tiresome upward journey, and reached the hacienda by moonlight.

"Our journey is over," said the Professor, "and it has been full and rich beyond my expectations. To-morrow we turn our faces homeward, having been absent nearly two months longer than we anticipated, but I, at least, have nothing but the pleasantest memories in connection with the tour."

"What of your long illness?" Maud asked.

"Have I not the deepest cause for gratitude in my wonderful restoration?—and think of the friends it brought me."

"I have certainly gained by the trip," Maud mused. "Health,

experience, a store of sketches — a real mine for future pictures — with friendships and pleasant memories."

Delight drew nearer to her father and clasped his hand, but said never a word. Nor did Victoria speak until she and Delight were curtained away from the night together. Then, as she combed out her long dark hair, she said, " My experience with the outside world has not been very satisfactory. I find that I cannot trust my own judgment to distinguish sterling metal from dross, and I am glad I am going back to Vassar for longer tutelage."

"I think I can guess what has vexed you," Delight replied, " but the Senhor was so very plausible and pleasant, I do not think you were in the least to blame for liking him a little."

"Like him!" Victoria exclaimed. " What is there in any person to like outside of *character?* and the Senhor showed himself, in so many little ways, mean, selfish, and despicable. If you could have heard how dishonorably he tried to prejudice me against Dr. Stillman."

" And Dr. Stillman was so thoroughly upright and self-sacrificing. He was really *good,* Victoria. I hope you did not wound him too deeply, for we all guessed when he went away that there was something the matter."

"Dr. Stillman was a saint, and I dare say I have hurt his feelings, but I can't help it, for, saint or sinner, I feel as if I never wanted to speak to another man as long as I live."

"O Victoria! you forget your father."

"So I did, and your father, and maybe one or two others; but what fools girls are to want to go into society before they have the least atom of sense in their little empty heads. I don't wonder that sensible women used to go into nunneries to escape marriage. For my part I would like to stay at Vassar for the rest of my days."

"I would not. The great beauty of Vassar to me is that it fits one for a busy and wider life. Look at Maud. She is an enthusiastic

Vassar girl, and yet she would no more like to go back there, and tread the old corridors and live the old life, than a chicken would like to shut itself up again in an egg-shell."

"Maud is a truly noble young woman, and she seems perfectly satisfied with being an old maid. Well, there are more resources for single women nowadays than formerly. They can do more, and can enjoy all the privileges of the age, as well as their married sisters. Delight, I have decided that I shall be an old maid, like Maud."

Delight laughed softly. "I will tell you a secret, Vic dear," she said.

"Well, what is it?"

"Maud is engaged."

"You don't mean it."

"I do, though; to a Mr. Richard Atchison, whom she met in England. He is a manufacturer somewhere in the Southern States."

"I never would have believed it of her; she is so downright sensible, and a Vassar girl too."

"Sensible people do marry sometimes, Vic, as I have no doubt you will some day. Maud's wedding is set for next Christmas, after her family return from Europe. If she gets the $5,000 reward for discovering the Senhor, it will be a nice little dowry, will it not? On reflection, I don't believe Maud would accept it. It seems too much like the price of a man's liberty."

"I don't see why she should hesitate. He deserves apprehension for his crimes. She deserves the reward for her shrewdness. If she does not take it I will make her a handsome wedding present, for I am very grateful to her for unmasking the villain in our little romance. And all the same, I am enormously disappointed in her, if what you say is true. Maud engaged — the idea!"

On leaving their friends, Philomena and Graciliano were offered the choice of having their expenses paid back to Santarem, or of receiving the same sum and entering into the service of Señor and

Señora Mirandella. They accepted the latter alternative, and the party left them established in a cottage near the hacienda.

Chimborazo, the glittering iceberg of the volcanoes, flashed like an opal in the morning sunshine, as they looked upon it for the last time. The land they were leaving was as beautiful as a vision, and yet there was a thrill in their hearts as they left it which was not all regret, and the old Professor, triumphant and happy as he certainly was, was humming under his breath, — what but " Home, Sweet Home!"

And was the defaulting Mr. Bartlett taken? And did Maud receive the reward? And did Victoria ever change her mind about the Doctor?

Pertinent questions all, — to be answered possibly in the future; but life is a continued story, which goes on and on, always linking itself into new incidents and situations, and never rounding all into completeness at any one time. I have given you their journey, a faithful transcript of all that befel our Three Vassar Girls in South America.

www.ingramcontent.com/pod-product-compliance
Lightning Source LLC
Chambersburg PA
CBHW031743230426
43669CB00007B/466